TITIUS AND BERTHA RIDE AGAIN:

Contemporary Moral Cases

Titius and Bertha Ride Again

CONTEMPORARY MORAL CASES

John F. Dedek

SHEED AND WARD, INC.
Subsidiary of Universal Press Syndicate

NEW YORK • LONDON

TITIUS AND BERTHA RIDE AGAIN. Copyright © by John F. Dedek. All rights reserved. Printed in the United States of America. No part of this book may be reproduced in any manner whatsoever without written permission except in the case of brief quotations embodied in critical articles and reviews. For information address: Sheed and Ward, Publishers, Inc., Subsidiary of Universal Press Syndicate, 475 Fifth Avenue, New York, N.Y. 10017

ISBN: 0-8362-0570-7 (cloth edition)
0-8362-0580-4 (paper bound)

LIBRARY OF CONGRESS CATALOG CARD: 74-1532

Contents

Preface 7
Case 1. Vasectomy and Artificial
    Insemination 11
Case 2. Invalid Marriages in the Internal
    Forum 25
Case 3. Baptizing Children of Lax
    Catholics 41
Case 4. Assisting at Abortions 49
Case 5. Homosexuality 57
Case 6. Sunday Mass....................71
Case 7. Cheating the Internal Revenue
    Service 81
Case 8. Passive Euthanasia 95

Contents

Case 9. Distributing Sparse Medical
              Resources 103
Case 10. Teenage Petting 111
Case 11. Clerical Obligations: Celibacy
              and the Breviary 119
Case 12. Devotional Confession 131
Case 13. Price Control and Demand
              Control..........................135

Preface

During the past decade the vast majority of books published in the area of Catholic moral theology have dealt with the more abstract questions that were traditionally treated by moralists in their tractates *De Principiis*. Fundamental issues concerning the nature of moral theology, natural law, situation ethics, human freedom, sin, personal responsibility, the formation and primacy of conscience, and so on have been the dominant themes. Some especially relevant practical issues like war, revolution, abortion, and drugs have also received considerable attention. But on the whole most

Preface

of the practical casuistry has been confined to the periodical literature and classroom lectures.

Traditional casuistry as it used to be practiced in the Catholic Church has rightly fallen into disrepute. The principal reason for this is that it pretended too much. It frequently tried to establish absolute practical norms that would cover every conceivable situation. No solution to a case can do that. No matter how concrete or specific it may be, a case still remains a universal. As a universal it can never replace the ultimate practical judgment of personal conscience in a unique existential situation. It can only serve to enlighten that personal decision of conscience.

Nonetheless, it is to the credit of the casuists of the past that they were willing to think a problem through and apply the general principles to concrete practical questions. The principles themselves, no matter how clear and profound they may be, are of little value unless they can be used to illumine the real problems of everyday life. What is more, the application of the principles to concrete cases frequently illumines the meaning of the principles in a way that was not seen before.

In the course of the renewal of moral theol-

Preface

ogy that has occurred since the Council, there have been some important refinements and a sharpening of our understanding of the traditional principles of Catholic moral theology. The necessary result has been some significant changes in the solution of some practical moral cases.

It is with this in mind that I have put together this short exercise in contemporary casuistry. Questions most frequently put to me during lectures given in the past year have largely determined my choice of the cases discussed here. As far as I can tell, they are questions very much on people's minds these days, especially the minds of parish priests who are directly engaged in ministering to the needs of Catholic people today.

The priest needs no introduction to the dramatis personae on the pages that follow. He is already well acquainted with Titius and Bertha, who were up to so much mischief on the pages of his seminary textbooks. Titius and Bertha are still engaged in a great deal of contemporary mischief, as you will see.

Case One

Vasectomy and Artificial Insemination

Titius and Bertha, both forty, have been married fifteen years and have five children. With the approval of her confessor Bertha has been taking oral contraceptives for the past year but recently has been experiencing some unpleasant side effects. Her family physician recommends that Titius have a vasectomy. He also suggests that before the operation Titius store some of his semen in a sperm bank so that later it would be possible for him to have another child by artificial insemination in case he might change his mind for some reason and want another

CASE ONE

child. Before making a decision Titius goes to his parish priest and asks his advice.

In his famous encyclical of 1968, *Humanae Vitae,* Pope Paul VI reaffirmed historic Catholic teaching that each and every marriage act must remain open to the transmission of life and therefore every act of contraceptive intercourse is intrinsically evil. In the same encyclical he said: "Equally to be excluded, as the teaching authority of the Church has frequently declared, is direct sterilization, whether perpetual or temporary, whether of the man or of the woman."

For a long time Catholic moral theologians tried manfully to defend these conclusions. But in recent years they have found them increasingly difficult to sustain. Contemporary moral analysis is still divided. But today, I think it is fair to say, a clear and decisive majority of Catholic moralists no longer support the traditional doctrine.

The new consensus does not deny that there is an essential connection between the procreative and love-union aspects of sexual intercourse. It affirms that these two aspects must be maintained in principle. Sexual intercourse

Vasectomy and Artificial Insemination

is not only love-making; it is also life-giving. God's creative love is mirrored in human procreative loving. As God's love is creative — he created nothing apart from his love — so we create new beings like ourselves in the midst of our love for one another. That is why sex is better than love: it is a special kind of love, the kind that is creative of new human life. To separate in principle the love-making and lifegiving aspects of sexual intercourse is to refuse the image of God's creative love in human procreative loving.

What this means is that sexual intercourse has an essential relationship to parenthood. But it does not mean that each individual act must be open to the transmission of life. The link between sex and parenthood is to be maintained. But it is not to be maintained blindly, leaving the decision whether or not to procreate new life entirely in the hands of chance or divine providence. Human parents must make responsible rational decisions about the number and spacing of their children. There may have been a time in human history when quantitative reproduction of the species was the paramount value. But today that is no longer so. Today quantitative reproduction is seen as

CASE ONE

a disvalue in our overpopulated world. The quality of life is now the most important consideration.

In the early sixties Catholic moralists began to question the Church's condemnation of oral contraceptives. Their analysis of the morality of the use of the pill forced them to enlarge their enquiry to every form or method of contraception. The majority conclusion at the end of the sixties was that the method used for contraception was morally irrelevant. Ethically it does not matter what method or technique is used for birth control. All that matters is that the link between human sexual love and parenthood not be broken in principle and that the practical decision about the number and spacing of children be made unselfishly and with responsible concern for the quality of engendered human life.

Linked with this new ethical analysis of contraception, and in some measure a result of it, was a new theology of dissent which was developed by Catholic ecclesiologists. Post-Vatican I ecclesiology held that no one might licitly disagree with an authoritative decision of the ordinary papal magisterium except an expert in the field who had uncovered some new evi-

Vasectomy and Artificial Insemination

dence in his research, and even he was only to suspend his judgment while he secretly brought the new evidence to the attention of the Holy See. Contemporary ecclesiology now affirms the right of any person to dissent from noninfallible decisions of the Church when he has sufficient reason for doing so.

Today a great many priests and lay people no longer have any problems of conscience about artificial birth control. They have decided that papal teaching on contraception is either erroneous or at least solidly doubtful, and they are supported in their judgment by the common dissent of contemporary Catholic theologians. But frequently they do not have the same security or clarity of conscience on the question of sterilization.

Perhaps the reason for their hesitation here is that this specific question has not undergone the same kind of public debate and widespread airing in the media. Or perhaps the reason is that most parish priests are not so clear themselves on this issue. In seminary textbooks sterilization was not treated together with contraception. It was treated as a separate question in a separate section of the manuals. Contraception was treated under the sixth command-

CASE ONE

ment as a sexual sin, whereas sterilization was treated under the fifth commandment as a sin of bodily mutilation.

The evil of sterilization, it was argued, is that it is an unlawful mutilation of our bodies, since it involves the suppression of the function of a very important bodily faculty, the faculty by which we procreate new life. In all cases other than sterilization, mutilation was permitted if it was in accord with the principle of totality. That is to say, mutilation was permissible if done for the good of the whole body. For instance, an amputation is moral only if it is done for the total health of the individual. Since an arm or a leg is given by God for the good of the whole body, it may be sacrificed only for the good of the whole body.

The same reasoning, however, could not be applied to sterilization, because, the moralists argued, unlike all other faculties and members of the human body, the sexual faculty is not given to us by God merely for the good of the whole body or individual person. The sexual faculty is given for the good of the species and so is not subordinated to the total good of any individual. The sexual faculty has a wider final-

Vasectomy and Artificial Insemination

ity: it is ordered to the good of the human race.

That is how the traditional argument against sterilization went. But when it was pressed, the real reason against it was disclosed. The question was raised: if the sexual faculty is for the good of the species, may it be surgically excised or may its function be suppressed when necessary for the good of the species, for instance in a population crisis? The response was negative. The reasoning: the sexual faculty is not for the good of the species in the sense that it is in any way subordinated to the common good or the good of society; rather, it is directly subordinated to God himself, the author of life.

Thus it became clear that the real objection to sterilization was the same as the objection to contraception in general. It interferes with the procreative purpose of sexual intercourse. Its fundamental evil is not that it is mutilation. If it were, it could be justified by the principle of totality. Its fundamental evil is that it is contraceptive mutilation. Hence even if it is necessary for the total good or health of the individual, it is still intrinsically evil and there-

CASE ONE

fore may not be willed, intended, or directly performed for any reason.

According to these principles only indirect sterilization was allowable. It was morally permissible, for instance, to remove a cancerous uterus, even though sterilization was a necessary but unintended consequence. But it was always forbidden to perform any surgical operation for the purpose of sterilization for any reason, even to protect the life or health of an individual or to safeguard any other important value. A good end never justifies an evil means. This is the theology contained in *Humanae Vitae,* in previous papal statements, and even in the American Bishops' recent *Ethical and Religious Directives for Catholic Health Facilities.*

Contemporary moral analysis has found this thinking too narrow. Sterilization that represents a rejection in principle of the relationship between human sexuality and parenthood is judged immoral. So is any form of contraception which would do the same thing. But sterilization done to protect some important value, for instance one's health, marriage, or the quality of human life, is morally evaluated in the same way as contraception in general.

Vasectomy and Artificial Insemination

This means that in contemporary ethical thinking there is no essential moral difference between sterilization and other methods of birth control. Sterilization is contraceptive mutilation. Insofar as it is mutilation it is governed by the principle of totality. Insofar as it is contraceptive it is governed by the same principles as contraception. As long as it does not negate in principle the connection between sex and parenthood, it is permissible for a proportionate reason.

There are, however, some very important practical differences. One is the relative permanence of sterilization. Today, after a vasectomy, recanalization is sometimes possible but the odds are not good. At the present time there is hardly more than a 50 percent chance that a vasectomy can be successfully undone. Dr. Joseph Davis, chairman of the New York Medical College Department of Urology, has announced experimentation with a "bionyx control," a microvalve which he describes as an "all metal truly reversible vasectomy device." It is a minuscule faucet-type valve made of gold and stainless steel and implanted in the male. It is installed in the "off" or closed position but later may be turned to the "on"

CASE ONE

or open position. But this is still in the experimental stage.

In our swiftly changing world permanent decisions are risky. A young couple ought to be rather cautious when thinking about sterilization. Because of the current wide publicity vasectomies are fashionable now. But being fashionable now could be a grave and often irreparable mistake for a young married couple.

Many couples do not realize that there are other means of contraception which are generally as effective as sterilization and do not entail any irreversible decision. For instance, the use of a diaphragm, together with spermicidal foam sprayed over the vagina from an aerosol can, is about 96 percent effective. Also the birth-control pill, properly used, is just as effective a means to prevent conception as a vasectomy. Because a woman experiences side effects, it does not automatically follow that she should therefore abandon the pill. Some of the side effects which women complain about are only trivial annoyances like headaches or some minor bleeding or spotting. I would think that a young woman generally would be well advised to put up with some of these nuisances

Vasectomy and Artificial Insemination

rather than have her husband undergo a probably irreversible operation.

An older couple, however, like Titius and Bertha might reasonably make a different decision. For them to terminate altogether and finally their reproductive capacity could more easily be considered a prudent decision. This aspect of the issue should be carefully weighed in any individual decision.

There are two other practical considerations which might be mentioned. One is that because of its permanence a vasectomy undergone before a marriage with the purpose of excluding all children would attack the *bonum prolis* in such a way as to affect the canonical validity of the marriage. The other practical consideration is the reported psychological effects that vasectomies sometimes have on a man. It is not easy to get any accurate information about this, but it seems that at least in some cases a vasectomized man experiences a loss of his sense of male identity or masculinity. As far as I can tell this is not a usual result, but since it may occur it should be at least a minor consideration as an individual tries to come to a practical decision.

In addition to sterilization there is another

CASE ONE

moral issue that Titius and Bertha have to resolve, the issue of artificial insemination. Should Titius store some of his semen in a sperm bank so that later, if he changes his mind, it would be possible for him to have another child of his own?

In 1897 the Holy Office decreed that artificial insemination is forbidden. And in 1949 and again in 1951 Pope Pius XII excluded the use of artificial insemination in marriage. The pope's fundamental argument against artificial insemination was rooted in the same principle as the argument against artificial contraception. Sexual intercourse is essentially a life-giving act of love-making and a love-making act of life-giving. It is an act of procreative love. That is its natural design, and to separate its procreative and love-union aspects is to violate the law of nature. Therefore both contraception and artificial insemination are wrong, because in contraception the procreative aspect is suppressed and in artificial insemination the love-union aspect is missing. As it is against the natural law to negate the procreative end of sexual intercourse in artificial birth control, so it is against the natural law to procreate apart from an act of love.

Vasectomy and Artificial Insemination

It is easy to see that these two arguments are perfectly consistent with each other and stand or fall together. One who dissents from papal teaching on contraception must logically dissent from papal teaching on artificial insemination, for these teachings are of a piece. If each individual act of sexual intercourse must be both love-making and life-giving, then artificial insemination is immoral even when the husband is the donor(AIH). But if contemporary moral analysis is correct in concluding that the procreative and love-union aspects must be maintained in principle but not in each individual act, then only insemination from another donor (AID) is excluded.

It might also be added that contemporary moralists would find no objection to masturbation as the means to obtain the husband's semen for deep-freeze storage. Traditional Catholic moral theology would never allow masturbation for any reason, since it, too, was judged intrinsically evil. But recent moral analysis no longer views the external act by which semen is obtained as constituting the moral entity of the action. Masturbation that is necessary for the artificial insemination of one's wife is no longer morally evaluated as a physi-

CASE ONE

cal or biological act. Rather the moral meaning of the physical act is determined by the circumstances and purpose toward which it is directed.

However, the practicality of Titius's plan to store some of his sperm in a bank is another question. Technologically, of course, it is possible. Sperm is mixed with glycerol, sealed in a bottle and frozen in liquid nitrogen at a temperature of minus 324 degrees Fahrenheit. When needed it is thawed and injected into the uterus. A large number of women have already been successfully inseminated with sperm that had been frozen for about two and a half years. But it is quite uncertain how long sperm can be preserved in this way. The last report I saw indicated that its effectiveness begins to diminish after two years or so. Certainly a young couple who planned to use frozen sperm many years in the future would have little assurance that their plan would work.

Case Two

Invalid Marriages in the Internal Forum

Titius and Bertha love one another deeply and have been happily married for sixteen years. They have five beautiful children, ages four, nine, ten, thirteen, and fifteen, all attending Catholic schools. Both parents are active in church and school affairs and attend Mass every Sunday with their children. But they do not receive the sacraments because they have been married in a civil ceremony. They were not able to be married in church because Titius had been married before. Both are very worried about their situation. In fact, Bertha already has been hos-

CASE TWO

pitalized because of a nervous breakdown. Yet they do not feel that they can sincerely promise to live together as brother and sister, nor do they think it would be right for them to break up their family and live apart. They go to their parish priest and ask his advice.

The *Code of Canon Law* declares that "marriage which is *ratum et consummatum* cannot be dissolved by any human power nor by any cause save death." This canon reflects Catholic teaching which has been practically unanimous and goes back to the earliest centuries. Although a few adaptations or compromises seem to have occurred in the history of the Church, in general the Fathers, Roman pontiffs, Church councils and synods made no compromise with secular law and practice. The rule was ancient, constant, and rigidly enforced: no divorce and remarriage.

To defend its strict teaching the Church has always pointed to certain Gospel texts in which Jesus is quoted as saying plainly that divorce and remarriage is adultery. Because of the ambiguity in Matthew's report, the question of the possibility of divorce and remar-

Invalid Marriages in the Internal Forum

riage in the case of adultery has been argued. But it seems fair to say that in the light of present-day knowledge and contemporary exegesis the best conclusion we can draw is that Jesus' teaching on divorce was truly radical and revolutionary. He rejected all divorce in principle and did not make an exception for adultery or anything else.

However, even if we accept this conclusion, it is long step to present-day canon law. Many contemporary exegetes argue that the saying of Jesus about divorce and remarriage is not a legal precept but a normative ideal. Jesus did not replace the divorce law of Deuteronomy with a new, more radical law for the New Testament. Jesus' saying about divorce and remarriage must be interpreted in the context in which it appears and not separated from that context. And the context in which it is put is the Sermon on the Mount, where Jesus was not making law but pointing to goals.

For instance, in the same context Jesus is reported as saying, "Do not resist the evil-doer; if a man strikes you on the cheek, turn to him the other." Almost all Christians have always interpreted this as a normative ideal, not a legal precept. It is a goal that Christians are bound

CASE TWO

to pursue. But it is not possible for it to be fully attained until the eschaton. In the meantime, while we are still a pilgrim people in a sinful world, it will be necessary sometimes to defend ourselves against unjust agressors.

The same, scholars of the Scripture argue, is true about divorce and remarriage. Jesus' norm is the goal toward which we must strive as a Christian people. But on the way we will always have to make adaptations or exceptions in impossible situations.

Other contemporary scholars argue that even if Jesus was making law, it is still a considerable distance from this to the doctrine contained in the *Code of Canon Law*. Even if Jesus is saying that divorce and remarriage is always sinful, it does not necessarily follow that the second marriage is invalid. According to this interpretation, a man who puts away his wife and marries another acts illegally but not invalidly. He commits a sin, but the sin is not unforgivable, nor does it exclude the possibility of a second valid union. Jesus may have been making law, but he was not making diriment impediments. It is canon law not the Gospel that declares the second marriage null.

Today the Church's traditional teaching that

Invalid Marriages in the Internal Forum

Christian marriage is absolutely indissoluble is also under heavy theological assault. We have never developed a genuine theology of marriage in the Catholic Church. Historically the sacrament of marriage fell almost exclusively into the hands of moralists and canon lawyers. The result has been that our understanding of marriage has been one-sidedly juridical.

Marriage is essentially defined in legal terms. It is defined as a contract. The principal official decisions that have shaped its understanding have been made by the tribunal of the Sacred Roman Rota, not the Biblical Commission or the Holy Office. And dogmatic theologians in their brief treatments of marriage generally have been content to repeat the principal conclusions of the jurists. For their own part, they have never developed a true doctrinal theology of Christian marriage. A few stammerings in this direction are beginning today, but no developed understanding or consensus has yet emerged.

The Church's traditional doctrine also is under increasing attack from lay people today. Since so many priests and religious have been released from their vows and allowed to marry, lay people frequently ask why in changing cir-

CASE TWO

cumstances a priest may be released from his life-long commitment made at ordination, while married people may never be released from theirs no matter what. The customary answer to this objection, of course, is that the priest is bound to celibacy by ecclesiastical law, whereas the married partners are bound to their commitment by divine law. The Church can dispense from her own laws but not from the laws of God.

Now, of course, Catholic exegetes and theologians are questioning whether the absolute indissolubility of Christian marriage really derives from divine law. Besides, there is a greater wisdom in this common lay objection than at first meets the eye. It is based on the common-sense perception that no human being is able to make an absolute commitment. Only an absolute being can make an absolute commitment. A human being can make a permanent commitment: that is what both priests and married people make. But in both cases it is made *humano modo*, not absolutely, since no one can foresee that circumstances or persons will not change in such a way as to make the fulfillment of the commitment impossible or immoral. One might argue against this that

Invalid Marriages in the Internal Forum

God, who requires absolute indissolubility, will in his providence give the grace making fulfillment possible and morally good in all circumstances. But that sort of argument is too aprioristic. The fact that divorce rates among Catholics approximate the general divorce rate suggests that God has a different policy.

In any event, interesting as all this speculation may be, the fact is that the official teaching of the Catholic Church remains the same today as always, and there is little reason to believe that this teaching will change in any substantial way in the forseeable future. So what is the parish priest to do in difficult pastoral situations like that of Titius and Bertha? Must he always unite canonical marital status with sacramental practice? Or can he sometimes counsel a couple whose marriage is not canonically valid to receive the sacraments without a head-on confrontation with ancient Catholic tradition and present-day canon law?

In trying to answer this question it will be helpful to distinguish two different cases. The first case is that of a couple whose first marriage was invalid but its invalidity cannot be proven in the ecclesiastical courts.

The ecclesiastical courts are useful and nec-

CASE TWO

essary institutions. They provide the social regulation of marriage that is necessary to keep the integrity of marriage and the imperative of permanence from being seriously endangered. Therefore, one ought to make use of the Church tribunals and follow their decisions in ordinary circumstances.

But it is also true that existing marriage law is imperfect and tribunal procedures are frequently cumbersome and severely limited. A negative decision (*Non constat de nullitate*) simply asserts that there is not full proof of the invalidity of the marriage. It does not assert that the marriage is certainly valid, and it cannot affirm this in many instances. The presumption in Church law is in favor of the validity of the marriage. But presumptions are not always in accord with the truth. It is quite possible that a person's first marriage was in fact invalid, and yet canonically its invalidity can never be affirmed at law.

Practically this means that when it is morally certain that a person's first marriage was in fact invalid but its invalidity cannot be proven at law, he may be licitly and validly married in a civil ceremony. Some authors draw the same conclusion when there is solid doubt about the

Invalid Marriages in the Internal Forum

validity of the first marriage. The reason for this is that a man has a natural right to marry once, and in the circumstances it is impossible for him to get married in the Catholic Church. He is unable to observe the prescribed canonical form for marriage, not because of any fault of his own, but because of the imperfection and limitations of the Church's legal system. In such circumstances the civil marriage would be licit and valid, and if the partners are baptized it would be a truly Christian sacramental marriage. The fact that it is not recognized canonically is simply a result of the necessary inadequacies of a human judicial process.

It is important to be clear that in these circumstances the civil marriage itself is a sacramental marriage. There is no need to have a second ceremony in the Church. If for some reason the couple would like to have a blessing-ceremony or renewal of vows before the priest, there is nothing to prevent this as long as scandal is avoided. But the priest should not perform the civil ceremony itself. John Catoir, the presiding judge of the Marriage Tribunal of the Diocese of Paterson, N.J., has wisely warned that "it would not be right for a priest to presume to marry the couple himself, i.e., to

CASE TWO

eliminate the need for a civil or religious ceremony outside the Church, because when acting as an agent of the state in the matter of marriage, the priest is under oath to obey the laws of the Church judicatory to which he belongs. If the priest knowingly witnesses a union which is juridically invalid in the eyes of his Church, he is exceeding his rights under state law as well as Church law, and even the civil validity of the marriage could be challenged later in certain states."

Finally, it is very important that this conclusion and the theological analysis which leads to it be widely publicized. It would be a mistake for it all to be kept very secret. Rather it can and should be explained to the people in the pulpit. For, as Richard McCormick has pointed out,". . . everyone writing on the problem of divorce and remarriage insists on the need of avoiding the scandal generated by misunderstanding. Catholics, therefore, must be educated to the idea that the tribunal system is severely limited in determining precisely what unions are truly binding and hence to the occasional legitimacy of internal-forum solutions. If they are properly educated, they will understand that there is no justification for shock or

Invalid Marriages in the Internal Forum

judgment when they see an acquaintance (divorced and remarried) receiving the sacraments. This education is particularly important for Anglo-Saxons, whose strong legal tradition accustoms them to view law as an exhaustive measure of what is possible and right. When this legal tradition combines with a highly juridical notion of Church, the result is the remarkable view that Church law provides the answer to all problems, the only answer and a fully adequate answer."

The second case is somewhat different and quite a bit more difficult. It is a marriage which includes a person whose first marriage was certainly valid but is now over, and whose second marriage is working out well. When the first marriage is now hopelessly broken (or dead, as some authors say) and the second marriage is established and involves children, there is a conflict of duties. One duty is to respect the indissolubility of marriage, and the other is to maintain the present love-community of the present family for the sake of the partners and the children.

An increasing number of moralists and canonists today maintain that the spouses should be able to continue to live together as husband

CASE TWO

and wife and receive the sacraments if scandal can be avoided. But there seem to be as many different reasons or arguments given for this conclusion as there are theologians who support it. This has to give us pause. That a clear consensus is forming on the correct pastoral practice is good reason for the parish priest to begin operating accordingly. But the fact that there is no clear agreement on the reasons that lead to the common conclusion indicates how very difficult it will be to explain such a practice to the people if it is adopted. And that, of course, is crucial if scandal is to be avoided.

Practically, therefore, at least at the present moment, I would recommend three things. First, I would not counsel couples in these circumstances to return to the sacraments on a regular basis at the present time. The principal reason for this is that I think it would be practically impossible to exclude serious scandal and harm to the Catholic community if a more relaxed practice developed just now. It would be very difficult for many Catholics to understand how divorce and remarriage is now permitted in one parish or by some priests and not permitted in another parish or by other priests.

Many good and loyal Catholics are still reel-

Invalid Marriages in the Internal Forum

ing after the birth-control controversy and its aftermath as well as all the other changes that have occurred since Vatican II. It would be pastorally insensitive to ignore the hurt and confusion that already has been caused them. I think that it would be next to impossible for many of them to assimilate such a drastic change in sacramental practice for divorced and remarried people unless they are given a very careful and thorough explanation. The problem is that the theological literature on this issue is still very young and groping. Solid and serious reasons have been advanced for a change in our sacramental practice. Almost everyone writing on the subject agrees that there should be a change. But there is as yet no agreement on the theological rationale for a change. The result is that it would be very difficult to formulate any clear and helpful explanation for the entire community at the present time. However, the literature is growing rapidly, and I suspect that a clearer picture will develop soon.

If there is a change in our sacramental practice, it cannot occur abruptly. Nor can it occur easily without official sanction and general guidelines from our bishops. Therefore it is most urgent that a national commission or at

CASE TWO

least diocesan commissions be set up to recommend some practical norms which will be universally followed in the local parishes and that a pastoral program of education of the people be inaugurated before any practical changes in policy are adopted.

I must admit that this is only my opinion. There are many good and responsible priests who are already operating more leniently, and they have good theologians to support them. All I am saying is that personally I think they are making a mistake and that if this mistake suddenly became widespread, serious harm would be done to the Church. One must sympathize with the agonizing cases of divorced and remarried couples like Bertha and Titius. But one must also be sensitive to the entire Church. It is not an easy matter to reverse a Church practice which has such a long and ancient history and about which feelings and emotions run very deep.

Second, I would be very careful in explaining to people why they should not receive the sacraments on a regular basis at the present time. Participation in the Eucharist is an objective sign of unity with the ecclesial community. The objective condition of a divorced and

Invalid Marriages in the Internal Forum

remarried person is a visible pattern of life at odds with the eccesial community and its beliefs about marriage. There is therefore an objective conflict between the sign-dimensions of the sacraments and the social conduct.

The fundamental reason, therefore, why a remarried person should not receive the sacraments is that their reception would be an objective external falsification of the significance of the sacrament. The reason is not that he is living in sin. No judgment is made or implied about his personal moral condition. It may well be God's will for him to continue in his present marriage, and he may well be living in God's grace as much as anyone else. It is important for people to understand that the Eucharist is not the only access to God. It is only one of many, which may happen to be closed to an individual for external reasons.

Finally, I would advise people in this difficult situation to come back to see me again in a year or so. I would not want to build up any false hopes. But I do think that in that time a clearer and more coherent theological consensus will have developed and a better practical solution may be able to be given.

Case Three

Baptising Children of Lax Catholics

Bertha calls the rectory to make arrangements for the baptism of her two-month-old baby. Her parents will be in town next Sunday, and she would like them to be the godparents since she is naming the baby after her father. Father Titius does not recognize her name and asks if she belongs to the parish. She tells him that she has been in the parish for two years but never registered because both she and her husband were married before and so could not get their marriage blessed in the Church. Further inquiry reveals that her husband has not gone to

CASE THREE

Mass since his divorce but that she always goes on Christmas, Palm Sunday, Easter, and several other times during the year when her parents are in town.

Father Titius explains that he is not sure whether he should baptize the baby since there seems to be little hope that he will be given a Catholic upbringing. Bertha argues that she has an eleven-year-old daughter from her first marriage and that she already has made her first Communion. Although her daughter has had no further religious instruction, she likes to go to Mass and goes with Bertha when she goes.

Father Titius is kind but firm. He explains that he cannot in conscience make a mockery of the sacraments. He cannot baptize the child and admit him into the Catholic religion when there is so little assurance that he will ever faithfully practice it.

In recent years some new prophets have arisen in the Church. They tell us that we are now living in a post-Christian era. They feel that most of the Christians in the world today are only nominal Christians, Christians by in-

Baptizing Children of Lax Catholics

heritance, custom, habit, and routine, not Christians by personal decision and deep commitment. In religion, they argue, it is quality not quantity that matters. It is far better for one truly believing Christian to go to Mass on Sunday in a secular city than for a whole village to attend Mass out of habit or routine. Therefore in the future we cannot put our hopes in large numbers. Christendom is dead. The Church of the future is the Church of the diaspora, a small but vigorous remnant of truly believing and practicing Christians who will be the tiny leaven in an unbelieving world. Numbers do not matter. What matters is that the salt of the earth not lose its own savor.

This new gospel tells us that the kingdom of God is like a king who gave a wedding feast for his son. The king said to the servants, "Select carefully an elite group of guests for my son's banquet." The servants drew up a list of only the good. And so the wedding hall had few banqueters.

It is of course true that there must always be an elite within the Church. But they are not the Church. The Church does not belong exclusively to an intellectual, moral, or spiritual

CASE THREE

elite. The Church of Jesus Christ belongs to the masses. And the masses are and always will be good, bad, and wishy-washy.

The Catholic Church is not called catholic by accident. The first heresy condemned by the primitive Church was Gnosticism, a belief that the large masses of Christians were not truly Christian, that the true Christians were a select group who had risen above the mediocrity of the crowd.

After its initial flirtation with Gnosticism the Church took seriously the command of Christ to spread the gospel to every creature. After all these centuries most of the world is still pagan and much more remains to be done. Nonetheless, something significant already has been done. Today more than 30 percent of the world's population bears the name of Christ. Most of these people are not saints, totally dedicated and committed Christians. But all of them at least have been baptized in the name of Jesus, bear his name, and are in touch with his saving word.

Much remains to be done in elevating the moral and spiritual level of those who profess faith in Christ. We cannot be triumphal, complacent, or content with massive numbers. But

Baptizing Children of Lax Catholics

neither may we escalate demands so that the Church is not in touch with the mass of mankind.

Becoming Christian is a process that we are all engaged in. It is of course possible to minimalize Christianity out of existence by having such minimal standards for admittance into the Church that we lose any significant ecclesial identity. But by escalating our demands it is also possible to maximalize it out of existence or at least out of the reach of the common man.

One Sunday after Mass a man introduced himself to me and said that he was a Quaker. He had come to Mass that Sunday with a Catholic friend. It was raining that day and so he had brought an umbrella, which he left in the vestibule during Mass. In his own church, he said, he always left his umbrella in the vestibule, and it was always there at the end of the service. Today he left his umbrella in the back of the Catholic church, and it was not there at the end of the service. Someone had stolen it.

At first I was very ashamed and embarrassed. What do you say to a man who complains that one of your parishioners stole his

CASE THREE

umbrella during Mass? But afterwards I thought that that is the way it must always be in a Catholic church.

Almost all the problems in the Church can be traced in some part to its size. Bigness tends to make our governance juricidal, our liturgy ritualistic, our clergy impersonal, and our people individualistic. But the alternative to universalism, to a religion for the masses, is elitism. And whatever else may be said for elitism, it is not a mark of the kingdom of God incarnated in the world of real men. The kingdom of God is like a king who gave a wedding feast for his son. The king said to the servants, "Go out in the byroads and invite to the wedding anyone you come upon." The servants went out into the byroads and rounded up everyone they met, bad as well as good. This filled the wedding hall with banqueters.

The Catholic Church has always been the church of the poor — not merely the economically poor, but those who are poor in faith, hope, love, chastity, justice, temperance, prudence, fidelity, veracity, and so on. The task of the minister is not to exclude these people from belonging. Rather his task is to guide them from poverty to greater richness, and to

Baptizing Children of Lax Catholics

do this gradually, step by step, not displeased at their distance from the goal, but pleased at the little progress they make.

If there were no prudent hope at all that Bertha's son would be given any religious education, Father Titius should not have baptized him at that time. He should not begin what will certainly never be completed. But in the case as described, there is certainly prudent hope of a Christian upbringing. Admittedly Bertha's standards are not very high. We would like considerably more. But we cannot demand more than we can realistically expect the masses of ordinary human beings to be able to attain. Jesus pointed to the highest ideals, but as a matter of fact he tolerated rather modest attainments even by his apostles.

Father Titius should have tried to meet personally with Bertha and her husband in an effort to persuade them to deepen their faith and religious life. He should have offered to give further instruction to their daughter so that she could make her confirmation. He should have investigated the possibility of validating their marriage. And, most of all, he should have entered their lives communicating his love for them and his approval of the good

CASE THREE

that is already in them, rather than communicating at the start his disapproval because of their sins. There are many things that he could and should have done to help them become better practicing Christians. But he should not have refused to baptize their baby because of their past failures and present limited attainments.

Case Four

Assisting at Abortions

Bertha, a registered nurse, works at the county hospital. She is assigned to work in the recovery room, where women who have an abortion are kept overnight under observation in case any complications develop after the operation. Titius, an intern, is assigned to give preoperative care to women who are to abort. The administration's policy is to excuse hospital personnel without recrimination from any work they object to for reasons of conscience. Both Titius and Bertha believe that abortion is immoral, and they are not sure whether their work makes

CASE FOUR

them accomplices. Bertha stops in to see her parish priest to ask his advice.

The legalizing of abortion has given rise to a new problem of conscience for some Catholic nurses, interns, and paramedical personnel working in public and non-Catholic health facilities. Should they cooperate in any way with the abortions that now are being performed in the hospitals and clinics in which they are working?

Those in charge of these health facilities are rightly concerned that every abortion be performed with maximum medical safety for the pregnant woman. Therefore, after the abortion they generally require the woman to stay for a time in a recovery room, where she will be kept under observation for possible postoperative complications like abscess, hemorrhage, and so on. Such complications are unusual, but if they develop they can present a severe threat to the woman's life. In that event, immediate attention by trained personnel is critically important.

Preoperative care is also important. Before the abortion an intern interviews and examines the woman to learn about any other diseases

Assisting at Abortions

she may have, to check her blood pressure, heart, lungs, and so forth, so that if any complications occur after the operation an accurate diagnosis can be promptly made. A surgical nurse is even more directly involved. Her job may be to set out the instruments, hand them to the doctor, and so on.

In some rare instances administrative policy has required interns, nurses, and paramedics to perform these services; and if they refused, they were fired or asked to resign. But even in the past such cases were unusual. Nowadays hospital personnel are generally given a free choice. If they ask to be excused from this work for reasons of conscience, the administration will honor their request and there will be no recrimination. In some places discriminatory hiring practices have shown up, and sometimes the official administrative policy is compromised by subtle pressures or punishment by particular individuals in charge. But in most cases the official policy is carried out in practice as meticulously and fairly as possible.

This is the context in which the moral question arises. What is the moral responsibility of those who believe that abortion is immoral? Should they participate in any way, or should

CASE FOUR

they ask to be excused for reasons of conscience?

In itself preoperative and postoperative care is morally good. It is the abortion that is immoral, not the medical care for the health and safety of the woman. This is exactly the same kind of care that an intern or nurse would give at a perfectly moral operation. The problem is that here it is not given at a perfectly moral operation. It is given in connection with an abortion.

If it is given with internal approval of the abortion, it is what theologians call formal cooperation, which is never permissible precisely because of one's internal approval of an immoral act. The formal cooperator is an accomplice who personally intends and wills not only the preoperative and postoperative care but the abortion as well. He shares in the blame for the abortion because of his bad will.

But it is quite possible for someone to give preoperative and postoperative care without approving of the abortion. Such care given without internal approval of the abortion is not formal cooperation. Rather it is called material cooperation. Material cooperation is permissible only if one manifests his disapproval

Assisting at Abortions

so as to prevent scandal and at the same time has a proportionately serious reason for cooperating.

Therefore, the difficult decision of conscience revolves around this question: do I have a proportionately serious reason for materially cooperating with an abortion? It is obvious at once that no universal answer can be given. The correct decision will depend on a complexity of competing values in the particular situation. However, some broad statements can be made to illustrate how Catholic moral theologians generally evaluate the issue.

Practically all theologians agree that material cooperation in an abortion would be justified if the intern or nurse were threatened with some serious harm, for example losing one's position with considerable personal loss. Also, many theologians argue that even if Catholic interns or nurses could get equally good or even better positions elsewhere, it does not follow necessarily that they should resign their positions at state institutions, since the spiritual and moral good they can do there may easily compensate for their occasional material assistance at an abortion.

In the present situation, however, loss of job

CASE FOUR

is seldom if ever an issue. Generally speaking, no one's job is on the line. In practically all health facilities individual decisions of conscience will be respected without recrimination. And normally no serious harm will be caused to anyone if Catholic nurses and interns ask to be excused from assisting at abortions. What this means is that ordinarily there will be no proportionate reason to justify their material cooperation in abortions.

Therefore, as a normal rule in the present circumstances Catholic nurses, interns, and paramedics should request to be excused for reasons of personal conscience from assisting at abortions in any way. Preoperative and postoperative care can easily be given by others who have no conscientious objections to abortion.

This rule, of course, is not absolute. Certainly there will be exceptions to it. Emergency situations will develop in which a Catholic would be morally obliged to give postoperative care to a woman in need of it. And there may be other considerations of good to be accomplished or harm to be avoided which in a particular situation would justify material assistance.

But in the absence of such serious reasons a

Assisting at Abortions

Catholic should abstain from any assistance directly connected with abortions. Although abortion is no longer a crime, it is still a sin. It is not enough for a Catholic merely to believe this internally. He should give visible witness to his convictions.

Hopefully, this common witness will say something to the medical profession and perhaps help sensitize others to the value of human life, whereas failure to give practical testimony could be scandalous, confirming the convictions of those who place less value on the lives of unborn children.

Case Five

Homosexuality

Titius is gay. Four years ago he was graduated from a Catholic high school and has not been inside a church since. After high school he got a job as an office clerk in the city, lives alone, and frequents the neighborhood gay bars where he makes a contact about once or twice a week. He used to be ashamed and secretive about his homosexual behavior but now is a gay liberationist, convinced that gay is good.

As a boy he was a devout Catholic but stopped going to the sacraments because he was unable to mend his homosexual ways. He has been deeply troubled about this, experiences a great loss in not being able to

CASE FIVE

practice his religion, and wonders if the Catholic Church has changed its views on homosexuality during the past few years. One day he gets his nerve up, stops at the rectory, and asks the priest if one has to be straight nowadays in order to be a practicing Catholic.

The meaning that one attaches to human sexuality will depend to a large extent on one's view of man. A dualistic anthropology, which thinks of man as a spiritual person who has a material body, will be inclined to undervalue man's sexuality. As we use our bodies, so we use our sexuality. Sex can be used for various purposes — for the expression of love and affection, for procreation, or for fun and pleasure.

But one who believes that man is his body, that he is the body of his soul as well as the soul of his body, will be more inclined to see the use of sex as expressive of his person. Sex is the way that he, who is his body, does the two most important things in life — love and create other beings like himself.

Human sexuality is both love-making and life-giving. That is its full human and Christian

Homosexuality

meaning, and anything less diminishes it. On the objective level homosexuality is something less. Homosexual acts are not life-giving acts of love. They separate in principle the love-union and procreative aspects of human sexuality. That is why Christians have always condemned them.

It is possible for two persons of the same sex to truly love one another in the deepest sense of the word. A genuine love relationship is more unusual between male homosexuals than between lesbians. It is at least statistically true that most male sexual relationships are casual affairs, and it is rare that they establish any kind of permanent bond rooted in interpersonal love. Female homosexuals, on the other hand, more frequently establish a permanent relationship based on genuine mutual love.

Nonetheless, a truly permanent loving relationship is not enough to fulfill the meaning of sexual communion. Good as love is, sexual union means more. Homosexuals may use sex to express love, but sex is better than that. Sex is more than an act of love. It is an act of creative love, an act by which we love and create new beings like ourselves.

An older theology exaggerated the impor-

CASE FIVE

tance of procreation and undervalued the importance of love. Procreation was seen as the primary end of sex, and any other values stood in a subordinate position. What we have to watch out for today is an overcorrection of this view, one which would dismiss procreation as if it were wholly irrelevant to the meaning of human sexuality.

Contemporary theological analysis no longer says that procreation is the principal purpose of sex, nor does it say that each and every act must be procreative or open to the transmission of life. It does not analyze our sexuality as a purely biological function. It sees it as a human function and says that as a human function it still has an essential relation to procreation.

Human sexuality is not just for loving. It is for a special kind of loving, the kind that is creative of new beings like ourselves. That is why it will always remain the *mysterium tremendum*. It represents and actualizes the best that is in us.

Homosexual acts necessarily exclude any relation to procreation, even the minimal relation that still exists in contraceptive or sterile heterosexual acts. Homosexual acts exclude in

Homosexuality

principle any reference to procreation and to that extent diminish the full meaning of human sexuality.

On the objective level, therefore, homosexuality will never measure up to or adequately reflect the full significance of human sexuality. This is true even of the best homosexual activity, that which is truly expressive of interpersonal love.

What is more, on the personal level, homosexuality can and frequently does depreciate the meaning of human sexuality in a further way. Often it is not even an expression of love. It is neither life-giving nor love-making. In such cases it is simply the selfish taking of venereal pleasure through the use of another person's body with the concomitant depersonalization of the other.

Men can fuck or they can make love. And *making love* is not just a euphemism for *fucking*. It describes a quite different human experience. One may "have sex" or "make love." He may "screw" or "have intercourse." He may "lay" someone or "go to bed." But all these expressions do not signify the same thing. An act of personal intimacy is one thing. Biological sex without feeling or caring is quite anoth-

CASE FIVE

er. Sexual intercourse is a sign of total unreserved giving of self. At the moment of orgasm the individual's personality is lost in an interpenetration of the other self. Sexual intercourse is expressive of one's person. To be authentic and not a lie it must correspond to the existing relationship between the persons. That is why fucking is morally wrong, even the fucking that is done by a faithful but unloving married couple.

Many homosexual acts, especially those among men, are in fact acts of depersonalized sex. They not only nullify in principle the procreative intent of human sexual love; they also regularly presuppose the absence of all emotional contact and responsible pledge.

To conclude, homosexual acts necessarily exclude all relation to procreation, and they frequently are not more than mechanical depersonalized acts of self-gratification. Human sexuality is better than that. That is why we cannot simply say that homosexuality is morally neutral, that it makes no difference whether one is homosexual or heterosexual, as if there were no important values or meaning at stake.

The preceding analysis is an attempt to isolate what is morally wrong with homosexuality

Homosexuality

on the level of ethical theory. It does not say that homosexuality is perverse or rotten or that anyone who engages in it is evil. It only says that it devalues the meaning of human sexuality in at least one and frequently two significant ways. This statement is made on the level of normative morality. It is important for one to be clear about it before he asks any other questions on the level of pastoral practice.

It is also important to be clear about another fact. Homosexuals are not born; they are made. And sometimes they can be unmade. Each of us finds his place somewhere on a homosexual-heterosexual continuum. Some people are exclusively heterosexual, some exclusively homosexual, and the rest somewhere in between. On a scale of one to seven, people can be classified as, (1) exclusively heterosexual, (2) predominantly heterosexual but incidentally homosexual, (3) predominantly but more than incidentally homosexual, (4) equally heterosexual and homosexual, (5) predominantly homosexual but more than incidentally heterosexual, (6) predominantly homosexual but incidentally heterosexual, and (7) exclusively homosexual.

CASE FIVE

People can be located on this scale according to either their psychic response or their actual behavior. In most cases overt behavior will follow psychic response. But in some instances one's actual behavior will differ from his psychic response. For instance, an inmate in a penitentiary or a boy in a military academy may be classified as predominantly heterosexual according to his psychic response but predominantly homosexual according to his actual behavior. One's psychic response, of course, is the more important factor, and apart from unusual circumstances it will determine one's overt behavior.

One cannot rule out the possibility that even a person who is exclusively homosexual can change sufficiently to live a normal heterosexual life. This is especially true if the homosexual is highly motivated. But there is only a very small likelihood of this happening. In fact there is only a small likelihood of substantial change by anyone whose psychic response has been either exclusively homosexual or predominantly homosexual and only incidentally heterosexual for a period of five to ten years. This does not imply that therapy has no value, only that it has limited value. Whenever possible it

Homosexuality

should be tried. Sometimes it will succeed at least in some useful degree. But more frequently it will fail, and nothing more can be done.

Lastly it should be noted that while the homosexual frequently is not free in determining his basic psychic response, he is usually free and in control of his actual behavior. His homosexual acts are not compulsive acts. Normally he has the same degree of personal control over his overt sexual behavior as a heterosexual person has over his.

With all the foregoing in mind, let us return to Titius and his parish priest.

The priest should try first of all to ascertain what exactly Titius means when he says that he is homosexual. Is he exclusively or almost exclusively homosexual in his psychic needs and response? Or is he able to switch? If he is able to behave heterosexually, then he ought to. It is not enough for him simply to say that gay is good and behave as if homosexuality were a morally indifferent matter. To freely choose homosexuality as a way of life when it is possible to do otherwise is a serious depreciation and mockery of the full human and Christian meaning of sex.

Second, if Titius cannot behave heterosex-

CASE FIVE

ually then ordinarily he ought to try to get some professional help. Therapy may or may not be useful. But usually it will be worth a try. In normal circumstances therapy would be ordinary means to protect some very important values. Therapy usually will require him to engage in physical intimacies with women, and I think that in the circumstances the priest could counsel this as the lesser evil.

But what if there is no way that Titius can change? What if he is irreformably homosexual in his psychic response and needs? This is the most difficult question, and it is being addressed in the theological literature in a very halting and exploratory way.

One tentative solution is that a confirmed homosexual may in his circumstances choose the lesser of two evils — namely, a permanent homosexual relationship built on mutual love rather than a life of casual promiscuity. He may do this only because for him heterosexuality is impossible and celibacy is not a truly viable option. Therefore, for him the lesser evil is the only possible good in the circumstances.

The weakness in this analysis is that it does not provide any solution for the many homosexuals who are unable to establish any perma-

Homosexuality

nent homosexual relationship built on mutual love and whose only choice therefore is between celibacy and casual promiscuity.

Another solution, based on the principle of compromise, asserts that because of the presence of sin and its effects in the world, homosexuality would not be objectively wrong in those circumstances in which it is the only viable alternative for an individual. Homosexual behavior will never be the ideal but can be reluctantly accepted as the only possible good, since it is the only way an individual can find a satisfying degree of humanity in his life.

It seems to me that this solution is not too bad as a practical pastoral norm but there is a certain amount of haziness in the theoretical principle that grounds it. I would suggest a somewhat different rationale which is a bit more precise and comes to the same practical conclusion. It is based on Schüller's preference-principle as refined by Joseph Fuchs. The principle states that premoral evil becomes moral evil only when done without a proportionate reason. Homosexual acts in themselves represent human disvalues in a premoral sense. They become moral evil in those circumstances in which there is no proportionate reason for

CASE FIVE

doing them. But if there is a proportionate reason for such acts, they remain premoral disvalues but not immoral even on the objective level. I would think that very often an individual's inability ever to engage in normal heterosexual acts would count as such a proportionate reason.

One might argue against all of these solutions that they too readily dismiss the possibility of celibacy and the power of God's grace. Maybe so. In any event the theological analysis of this question is far from complete, and as far as I can tell no significant consensus has been reached.

Even if a pastor is unable to accept any of the theoretical solutions outlined above, he still can handle the case on subjective grounds in the following way. If Titius can switch to heterosexual behavior but does not, he is freely choosing homosexuality as a way of life and so choosing to depreciate and trivialize the meaning of human sexuality in a significant way. Such a decision, I think, would be seriously wrong and would make him undisposed to receive the sacraments fruitfully.

But if Titius is irreformably homosexual and tries with ordinary diligence to abstain from

Homosexuality

homosexual behavior, he can be treated pastorally in much the same way as an adolescent masturbator. For if he has not freely chosen homosexuality as a way of life and yet periodically fails because of his limited options, these single acts of homosexuality probably would not be gravely sinful. And even if they were, his effort to resist them would evidence sufficient disposition for sacramental absolution.

Case Six

Sunday Mass

Bertha, a first-year college student, is home for her Christmas vacation. A few days before Christmas she stops at the rectory and tells the parish priest that while away at school she has stopped going to Sunday Mass. Occasionally on a weekday evening she has gone to a small group Mass at the Newman Center and has found this an authentic religious experience. But she cannot say the same for the typical Sunday Mass in the parish church. She honestly feels that regular Sunday Mass is not a meaningful religious experience for her, that she gets nothing out of it, and that many who do go every Sunday are really hypocritical, going

CASE SIX

> *through empty ritual out of fear, habit, routine, or a need for social approval.*
>
> *This brings her to her present problem. She does not want to be a hypocrite by going to Mass with her parents while on vacation just to please them. At the same time she knows that they will be deeply hurt if she tells them that she does not go to Sunday Mass any more.*

The sensitive counsellor will listen carefully to Bertha in an effort to determine her real question. Perhaps the problem is precisely and simply the one she poses. He will not discount this possibility on the assumption that it is necessarily deeper. But perhaps it is deeper. She may be reacting to something else — her past religious training, her new self-image, social pressures in her new environment, a problem of faith, her own growing up, repressed resentment and anger at her parents, a sense of guilt about her current sexual behavior, or what not.

Some of these things may surface in a leisurely counseling session. But even if the question Bertha poses is not the whole problem or the most important problem, it is still a valid

Sunday Mass

question and cannot be dismissed as if it is no issue at all. In some situations where the deeper issue is surfaced and resolved, the problem about Sunday Mass may simply disappear. But in other situations it will remain a question to be dealt with on its own terms.

In talking with Bertha the priest should be clear in his own mind on at least three things: (1) the meaning of Sunday Mass, (2) the necessary limits of this meaning, and (3) the current theological teaching on the canonico-moral obligation of Sunday Mass. The priest himself will have to judge how much of this it will be pastorally opportune to say to Bertha in the particular situation.

1. *The Meaning of Sunday Mass.* The Apostles began to celebrate the new religion of Jesus on the first rather than the last day of the week. In the first epistle to the Corinthians and in the Acts of the Apostles we read that St. Paul met with the people on the first day of the week for the breaking of the bread. In the Apocalypse St. John is already calling Sunday "the Lord's Day." The early Christians called Sunday the Lord's Day because it was the day on which Jesus after his death proved himself to be the Lord.

CASE SIX

From then on, Sunday was the Day of Christ the Lord. In Greek it was called *Kyriake,* in Latin *Dies Dominica.* And so our calendars came to be marked. In all the Romance languages the first day of the week is called the Lord's Day: in French *Dimanche, Italian Domenica,* Spanish *Domingo.* Only in the Teutonic languages is the pre-Christian name of Sunday retained.

In the year 150 St. Justin described a typical Sunday. Christians from the city and country came together; Scripture was read, especially the Gospels; petitions were offered; bread and wine were brought up to the altar; the solemn prayer of eucharist was said and the bread and wine were transformed into the body and blood of the Lord, and then all present received a share. That was the Christian Sunday in the second century. The divine service was substantially identical to the Mass of today.

During the persecution of Diocletian, Christians were charged with holding their own special religious services. In the Roman Empire one could hold any religious beliefs or philosophical theories he wanted. What was illegal and punishable at law was to hold one's own religious services. Still the Christians persisted,

Sunday Mass

telling the authorities when brought to trial, "Sine Dominico non possumus — we cannot live without celebrating the Lord's Day."

At the Last Supper Jesus told his disciples, "Do this in memory of me." This is the meaning and purpose of the Christian Sunday — keeping alive the memory of the Lord. Christians will do this until he comes again, and they will do it on the Day of the Lord.

2. *The Limits of This Meaning.* One often hears young people today saying that Sunday Mass is not a meaningful experience for them, that they do not get anything out of it. They get more by praying to God alone, at home or under the stars.

What must be said in response is that Mass can never replace private prayer and is not meant to. Each person is unique and has a unique relationship with God. This uniqueness can be reflected only in private prayer.

However, we are not only unique individuals. We are also a people. We are structured into a community which exists in a certain geographical place and moment of history. And so we relate to God as a people, not only in our aloneness. This means that just as Mass can never replace private personal prayer, nei-

CASE SIX

ther can private personal prayer ever replace the Mass.

The idealism of youth frequently expects too much and so is necessarily disappointed. Mass will never capture one's total religious experience nor satisfy all of one's religious needs. It is a limited good with a limited purpose. Mass is only Mass; it is not everything. And no amount of liturgical reform, guitars, or new and better music can make it everything. One who raises his expectations beyond reasonable limits is bound to be disappointed.

Each year the young deacons who have spent six months in a parish return to the seminary for a short time before their ordination to the priesthood. Recently a group of them were expressing their disillusionment with the funeral services they had been involved in. The common complaint was that often, especially in the large city parishes, they did not even know the person they were burying or any of the immediate family. And so they found their function at wakes and funerals intolerably impersonal.

I told them that personalism is not the only value in life, nor is it the yardstick by which

Sunday Mass

everything else is measured. Liturgy and ritual are only liturgy and ritual. They have a useful but limited function. On the occasion of death the Church stands up and proclaims in a ritual way the Christian belief that death is swallowed up in victory. This does not bring the same comfort to the family as the sympathy of a personal friend. But it brings some comfort, comfort of a sort that personal friends cannot bring. Ritual and liturgy are useful and supply a genuine need. They are not everything, but one should not conclude that therefore they are nothing. It is a mark of maturity to recognize and appreciate limited goods for what they are.

The same must be said about Sunday Mass. It is not the only thing and it is not everything. But it is something — something which has been, is, and always will be important in the Christian life.

3. *The Juridical Obligation.* One frequently hears it said today that missing Mass on Sunday is no longer a mortal sin. This is not exactly true, and it is not exactly false.

Canon 1248 reads: "Mass is to be heard on prescribed feasts." The prescribed feasts in-

CASE SIX

clude all the Sundays of the year. This law has not been abrogated by the Church and is still binding on Catholics.

In the past, theologians and canonists unanimously interpreted this law as prescribing an important observance and consequently entailing a serious obligation in conscience. The common casuistry acknowledged that one could come late or miss certain parts of the Mass and only sin venially, but to miss more than one-third of the Mass on a single Sunday was a grave omission. It also acknowledged the possibility of legitimate excuses. A moderately grave inconvenience would excuse one from the obligation on a particular Sunday.

Today moralists and canon lawyers generally are taking a different approach. They no longer judge that missing more than one-third of a Mass is grave matter. Rather they say that the "substantial nonobservance" of the precept is grave.

The principle of substantial observance was first articulated in connection with Pople Paul VI's *Paenitemini* in 1966. *Paenitemini* abrogated the old laws on fast and abstinence and instituted the present discipline. When it was released *Osservatore Romano* issued a semiof-

Sunday Mass

ficial commentary which explained the notion of substantial observance. It pointed out that the laws on fast and abstinence externalize the interior obligation of penance that binds all of us sinners. But single infractions of the external law do not undercut the whole spirit or purpose of the law. Individual violations do not nullify the value being protected by the law, namely the value of personal repentance. Therefore, the commentary concluded, the faithful should be instructed that the general neglect of the law would be grave but not individual violations.

From this new explanation of the binding force of ecclesiastical laws on fast and abstinence moralists today have drawn a further conclusion: the same principle of substantial observance must apply to every positive law of the Church which enjoins a practice. So the practice of attending Sunday Mass must be subject to the understanding that one does not nullify the whole spirit of the law if one does not obey it on one or another occasion. What this means is that Catholics still have a juridical obligation to attend Sunday Mass. The general or substantial neglect of this obligation is grave, but individual violations are not.

Case Seven

Cheating the Internal Revenue Service

Doctor Titius, an orthodontist, has successfully hidden about one-fourth of his annual income from the IRS during the past ten years. Last year he was called in for an audit. The agent was suspicious about his return, harassed him for a while, but was unable to uncover any hard evidence that Titius was cheating.

The investigation made Titius very nervous, and although he escaped criminal prosecution he is now having problems of conscience. On Saturday afternoon he goes to confession, tells the priest that he has been

CASE SEVEN

cheating the IRS for ten years, and asks if he is morally obliged to make restitution of his back taxes.

In recent times most moralists have judged that an individual's obligation to pay taxes was governed by the canons of legal justice. But in the past many theologians held that the individual citizen has a strict obligation in commutative justice to pay all just taxes. For, they argued, there is an implicit contract between the government and the people: the government is to provide public goods and services and the people are to pay their fair share in support of them.

St. Alphonsus Ligouri cited twenty-three authors who held this opinion and said that it was the most common and probable one in his day. And in the present century this view has had some support. For instance, Dominic Prümmer wrote: "Without the payment of just taxes social life today would be almost impossible. In return for his taxes the government provides the citizen most precious benefits — internal and external peace, roads, recreation centers, postal service, etc. All these things are not given free. Hence if citizens refuse to pay

Cheating the Internal Revenue Service

their just taxes and still accept these benefits they violate commutative justice."

At least on the level of federal tax laws, this opinion no longer has any probability. Anyone who understands the true purpose and function of federal tax legislation as it exists and is understood in our contemporary economic and political society has to dismiss this ethical view as wholly obsolete. It may have been defensible in a feudal society. It may sound convincing to one who is unaquainted with the new economics. But it certainly has no relevance to the real economic world in which we currently live. The correct ethical evaluation of this complex issue will be considerably illumined by an accurate understanding of the contemporary meaning and purpose of taxation in the modern economic state.

In 1883, the year that Karl Marx died, John Maynard Keynes was born. He became a Cambridge don, lecturing on economics. In 1935 he wrote a letter to George Bernard Shaw saying, "I believe myself to be writing a book on economic theory which will largely revolutionize — not I suppose at once, but in the course of the next ten years — the way the world thinks about economic problems. . . . I cannot

CASE SEVEN

expect you or anyone else to believe this at the present stage. But for myself I don't merely hope what I say — in my own mind, I'm quite sure."

Not only was he quite sure; he was quite right. No other book — neither *Wealth of Nations* nor *Das Kapital* — has so decisively turned economics upside down as Keynes's *The General Theory of Employment, Interest, and Money*. Thirty-five years later *Time* magazine was quite accurate in saying, "We are all Keynesians now."

It took a long time for his theory to be adopted in political and economic practice. The principal reason is that his book is almost inscrutable. Here is a typical sentence: "Let Z be the aggregate supply price of the output from employing N men, the relationship between Z and N being written $Z = \phi(N)$, which can be called the Aggregate Supply Function." If economics had not already been known as the dismal science, it would have after Keynes. His book has been described as a tractless desert of economics, algebra, differential calculus, and abstraction.

Nonetheless, from 1936 on, while the old economics was still taught in the schools by

Cheating the Internal Revenue Service

day, in the evenings almost everyone discussed Keynes. What saved *The General Theory* from premature internment was the fact that the messiah had able and lucid prophets: Alvin Hansen and Seymour Harris of Harvard, Paul Samuelson of MIT, a group of younger economists at the University of Chicago and Yale, and more recently John Kenneth Galbraith and Walter Heller. The result of their efforts has been that today Keynesianism is the new orthodoxy.

Canada was probably the first country to put Keynes's theory into practice. The Eisenhower administration tried it during the recession of 1958 and it worked. Presidents Kennedy, Johnson, and Nixon have continued its use, and it has now become our standard economic policy.

Simply put, the new economics says: "If unemployment and idle productive capactiy persists in an advanced economy, this evil can be cured by manipulation of government spending and taxation — more spending or less taxation to increase total demand in the economy. In these circumstances the fact of a deficity in the budget is irrelevant. Spending more and taxing less will actually reduce the deficit

CASE SEVEN

by creating more production and jobs and hence more revenue."

Therefore President Roosevelt did exactly the wrong thing during the Great Depression. His policy of "pump-priming" poured money into the economy, but his increased taxation to pay the deficit took it out again. And so he prolonged the Depression needlessly. It was overcome only by the great deficit financing necessary for World War II. The Keynesian secret, therefore, is deficit financing — more government spending or a cut in taxes — during a recession, and a surplus — less spending or increased taxation — to prevent or slow down inflation.

Milton Friedman of the University of Chicago has convinced many economists that the manipulation of the national economy by tax increases or reductions must go hand in hand with a complementary monetary policy. A tight money policy offsets the effects of a tax cut. In 1964 the fiscal policy, a tax cut, and the monetary policy, the supply of credit or money from the Federal Reserve, moved in the same direction with favorable results. But in 1966 a budget deficit was counterbalanced by a decrease in the money supply. The result was

Cheating the Internal Revenue Service

the mini-recession of 1967, which was finally corrected only by reversing the tight money policy.

Also, John Kenneth Galbraith has argued persuasively that fiscal policy sometimes must be combined with wage-price controls if we want nearly full employment at all times, since Keynes's fiscal policy of keeping a balanced and steadily growing economy through tax regulation assumes that there can never be full employment.

These two corrections have been nuances or complements of the basic Keynesian doctrine. But with these qualifications, it seems safe to say that Keynesian theory has won the day and explains the true purpose and function of federal taxation. The federal government does not tax us to raise revenue to pay for government's goods and services or to balance its budget. Rather, taxation is the instrument for the manipulation, regulation, and fine-tuning of our general economy. In the process it also redistributes the wealth among the people for the sake of the general economic well being.

The conventional wisdom and some of the political rhetoric still assume that the federal government has to pay its bills just like every-

87

CASE SEVEN

one else. Nothing is further from the truth. The fact is that there is no way for us ever to pay off our national debt and there is no reason why we should ever do so. The failure of the conventional wisdom is that it likens the national debt to personal debt, but this comparison is wholly misleading. International debt may bear some similarity to personal debt, but the national debt is quite different.

The difference is that when one incurs a personal debt, say, by buying a house with a long-term mortgage, one is able to consume more now than one earns or produces. But when a nation incurs a national debt, it is not able to consume any more than it earns or produces. There is no loosening of the belt by incurring the debt and so no need to tighten it afterwards.

Personal debt always makes one poorer, for one's net worth equals one's assets less one's debts. But national debt does not make a nation any poorer, because national debt plus national credit equals zero. A national debt of one trillion dollars means a national credit of one trillion dollars. A national debt of one trillion dollars does not make us poorer by a trillion dollars any more than a national credit

Cheating the Internal Revenue Service

of one trillion dollars makes us that much richer. We are as rich or poor as our gross national product. The national debt and national credit cancel each other out, for the simple reason that we owe the national debt to ourselves.

This means that we never have to pay our national debt no matter how big it gets. It is true that government bonds and treasury certificates fall due on certain dates. But then new bonds and notes can be issued and often to the same people who held the original certificates which matured. For it is to the benefit of people with extra money to invest it in interest-producing certificates rather than to hold it in nonproductive cash.

The result, of course, is that we are always sinking deeper into debt, because the interest payments alone have become an enormous government expense. But this can go on forever, since we can keep borrowing money to pay the interest. All this does is increase the national debt, which does no harm in itself.

But, one wonders, what if everyone lost confidence in the government at once and wanted his money now? First of all, that is impossible as long as there is no national econ-

CASE SEVEN

omic disaster such as the Great Depression (and, thanks to Keynes, that also is impossible now). But suppose it were possible and did happen. Then the government could print money instead of bonds and treasury certificates if, for some unimaginable reason, all the people preferred to hold currency which does not yield any interest.

Then why do we not simply cancel the national debt if it does not matter? The answer is that it does matter, but not in the way or with the effect that the conventional wisdom thinks. When we say that we owe the national debt to ourselves, the *we* and the *ourselves* do not designate the same individuals. Therefore, if we simply canceled the national debt, the richer people who hold most of the government securities would be hurt (although they would be considerably compensated because the accompanying reduction of taxes would help them much more than the poor).

Besides, the people who own the national debt, that is, the creditors, are and feel richer. Hence they spend more, since they already have a lot of money in savings. Their extra spending is good or bad depending on the current state of the economy. If there is a

Cheating the Internal Revenue Service

recession, the spending is good; if there is inflation, the spending is bad. That brings us back to the real meaning and function of federal taxation today. It is for the fine-tuning of the overall economy, to check recession and control inflation, by keeping an appropriate amount of money and consequent purchasing power in the hands of the people at all times.

Practically, what all this means is that the individual citizen has no obligation in commutative justice to pay his federal income tax and therefore no moral obligation to make restitution if he fails to do so. An obligation to restitution does not arise from a violation of social, legal, or distributive justice. It arises only from a violation of strict commutative justice, and there is certainly no question of commutative justice here.

This, of course, is no novel moral opinion. Even theologians working out of the old economics held that in practice one could in good conscience follow this opinion. Some theologians in the past believed that there was an obligation in commutative justice, but many others argued that the obligation arose rather from legal justice. Because of the dispute among moralists, there was prudent doubt and

CASE SEVEN

so, thanks to the doctrine of probabilism, the more lenient opinion could be used. Today, thanks to our understanding of the new economics, we need no longer have recourse to probabilism and prudent doubts. We are certain that the stricter opinion has no foundation and is of historical interest only.

The function of federal taxation is not the collection of revenue to balance its budget. It is not an effort to have every citizen pay his fair share for government goods and services. Hence, the issue is not one of an individual defrauding others in the society by not contributing his allotted share to pay for the common benefits. That is the image in the conventional wisdom, but it is not what is going on. Rather, the purpose of modern federal taxation is to control and manipulate our economic system for its general well-being. To this end it redistributes the wealth and adds or subtracts money from the economy according to the current economic conditions. It achieves this goal by enacting and enforcing appropriate tax legislation.

This legislation certainly does not suppose or give rise to any obligation in commutative justice or to any obligation to restitution in

Cheating the Internal Revenue Service

instances of its violation. And whether it gives rise to any moral obligation at all is still an open question. An increasing number of contemporary moralists are denying the existence of purely penal laws, arguing that every just civil law binds in conscience. But I think that it is safe to say that even this issue is still debatable and, therefore, in practice one may follow the more lenient view.

In the case of Dr. Titius, therefore, the confessor should briefly explain the nature and purpose of modern tax laws, not urge any moral obligations which are doubtful, and certainly not suggest restitution because of his fraudulent returns in the past.

Case Eight

Passive Euthanasia

Titius, age fifty-five, has had diabetes for twelve years. During this time he has kept the disease under control by giving himself regular injections of insulin, and so has been able to live a normal and productive life as a high-school teacher. Now, however, exploratory surgery has disclosed that he has an incurable cancer of the bowel, and in the judgment of the surgeon he has about six months to live. Titius dreads the pain, expense, and humiliation of dying slowly of cancer of the bowel. He and his wife consult the hospital chaplain about the possibility of discontinuing his insulin shots so that he will die quickly and more peacefully in a diabetic coma.

CASE EIGHT

A question receiving considerable attention these days is: What means ought to be used to keep a person alive? The question usually takes this form: When should a physician turn on or turn off a heart-lung machine, begin or not begin, continue or discontinue artificial respiration, oxygen, intravenous drip, and so on? Closely allied to this question is another: If a patient has two fatal diseases, one curable and the other not, should the physician continue to treat the curable disease? For instance, should a physician always treat and cure pneumonia in an aged and senile patient? Or should a physician prescribe insulin for a terminal cancer patient who develops diabetes? Or must a diabetic patient who develops terminal cancer continue his insulin injections?

There is of course the absolutist view, more common among physicians than moralists, that a doctor must make every possible effort to keep a person alive. For instance, he must use every means available to stretch out the life of a terminal cancer patient to the very end. According to this view a physician's duty is to cure disease and to do this relentlessly even when the patient cannot be finally cured. He must carry on the fight against death until the issue is taken out of his hands.

Passive Euthanasia

The position of traditional medical ethics commonly has more nuances. Medical ethics as it developed in the West introduced the more flexible categories of ordinary and extraordinary means. The majority of ethicists argued and still argue that only ordinary means must be used to preserve life and that extraordinary means are elective, not mandatory. Pope Pius XII, who has not gone down in history as a crusading liberal in the area of medical ethics, personally confirmed this moral teaching.

These terms — *ordinary* and *extraordinary means* — are familiar, but a difficulty often lies in their ambiguity. There is generally a significant difference in the meaning of these terms as they are used by physicians and moralists.

The physician usually considers ordinary whatever means are standard, orthodox, or established medicines or procedures within the limits of availability. He considers extraordinary a medicament or procedure that is fanciful, bizarre, experimental, incompletely established, unorthodox, or not recognized.

For the moralist, on the other hand, the ordinariness of the means is simply measured by two factors — its convenience and utility. Therefore the moralist defines ordinary means as not only normal food, drink, and rest but

CASE EIGHT

also all medicines, treatments, and operations which offer a reasonable hope of benefit and which can be obtained without excessive expense, pain, or other inconvenience. He defines as extraordinary means all medicines, treatments, and operations which cannot be obtained without excessive expense, pain, or other inconvenience for the patient, or which if used would not offer a reasonable hope of benefit to the patient.

This last point is most important. In determining which means are to be counted as ordinary and which as extraordinary, their usefulness is as decisive as their convenience. Even means that generally are classified as ordinary should be counted as extraordinary if their use will confer no significant benefit on the patient.

Take, for instance, a man with terminal bone cancer, who is conscious, gets only brief relief from pain-killing drugs, and will live for several more weeks unless someone pulls the plug on the artificial respirator and removes the tubes for intravenous feeding. In the view of the ethicists these normal aids are to be judged extraordinary means in the circumstances, since they are not useful means to save

Passive Euthanasia

life. Their continued use confers no significant benefit on the patient. They do not significantly prolong life. Rather they needlessly and torturously prolong the process of dying.

There is often another important difference in the perspective of the physician and that of the moralists. The physician as a scientist is inclined to see his task as treating and curing diseases. The moralist, who is not a scientist, gives the physician a somewhat different job description. The physician's mission is to cure people and save their lives. His job is patient-centered, not disease-centered. As Paul Ramsey once observed, "Doctors do not treat diseases, though they often conquer them. They treat patients, and here finally all fail."

This subtle nuance in perspective makes a great practical difference. Take the case of a patient who has two fatal diseases, one which can be checked and another which is terminal, for instance a terminal cancer patient who develops diabetes or a diabetic patient who develops an incurable cancer. Is the physician obliged to treat the diabetes, or is the patient obliged to continue on insulin, so that he will die slowly of cancer rather than sooner and more easily in a diabetic coma? Or similarly,

CASE EIGHT

what must be done for a slowly deteriorating senile old man who develops pneumonia? Must he be given antibiotics to cure the disease which has long been known as the old man's friend?

In these and similar cases the ethical conclusion is that the disease which may be cured or checked need not be treated. The reason is simply that the treatment in such circumstances is not a useful remedy. The treatment will halt one of the diseases. But it will not confer significant benefit on the patient. The subject of medical treatment is the patient who has two diseases. It is not the individual diseases one be one; only a narrowly scientific view would say it is.

In deciding whether one is obliged to use insulin for diabetes or antibiotics for pneumonia one cannot merely ask whether the treatment will cure or check the disease. One must ask whether the treatment will be useful and beneficial for the patient whose dying has already taken irreversible control. One does not realistically prescind from an advanced and terminal cancer in answering that question.

It is, of course, first of all the right of the patient himself, not the doctor, to decide

Passive Euthanasia

whether extraordinary measures should be initiated or discontinued. If the patient is conscious and rational, that is, able to understand and evaluate the situation, it is up to him to decide the issue, and the doctor should respect his wishes.

But if the patient is unconscious or unable to rationally decide, theoretically his nearest kin should make the decision for him. Practically, however, the relatives are often the worst judges of what should be done when someone they love is dying. The immediate family often feels enormous guilt, not because of what they have done in the past but because of what they imagine they should or might have done to show the love they now so keenly feel. As a result they want everything possible done for him now. They want to prolong his living to the last possible moment and beyond any reasonable moral warrant. They cannot bear the added guilt that would come from a decision to discontinue any means that might delay the death of the one they love.

In such a situation it can easily become the responsibility of the doctor to take the lead in suggesting what should and what should not be done, what in his judgment would be best for

CASE EIGHT

the dying man. In this way he can help the family come to the right decision and reduce considerably the burden of a decision which otherwise they could not bear. Also there will be situations in which the family cannot or should not be consulted. Then the doctor will have to make the decision himself according to what he judges is in the best interest of the patient.

Case Nine

Distributing Sparse Medical Resources

At County Hospital there are ten patients in need of hemodyalisis. At present only six can be accommodated on the kidney machine. The other four cannot be treated and must be left to die. The hospital administration has no medical criteria on which to decide who should live and who should die. So they set up a lay board to make the decision anonymously. The board is given only the following information about the patients: (1) age, (2) sex, (3) marital status, (4) number of dependent children, (5) occupation, (6) annual income, and (7) net

CASE NINE

worth. The board meets and wonders what criteria should be used in making this kind of decision.

The problem of the equitable distribution of sparse medical resources will always be with us in one form or another. One instance that is still causing concern even in some sections of our own country is hemodyalisis. If there are more people in need of hemodyalisis than can be accommodated on the kidney machines, who should receive the treatments and who should be allowed to die? What criteria does one use in making such a decision?

There is of course a more fundamental question here which I shall not try to answer. It is the question of determining our societal priorities. As Leibniz said, "All things are possible but all things are not compossible." We may be able to do anything but we are not able to do everything. And so one question that arises is: Should the medical profession be in the business of hemodyalisis at all? Could the enormous amount of money and professional talent spent on hemodyalisis each year better be used in research calculated to prevent kidney diseases?

Distributing Sparse Medical Resources

I do not know the answer to this question or to the more general question of the priorities in allocating the large but limited resources of our society. I only bring it up because it is the basic issue and should not be decided by indecision but by rational social planning. In any event, let us get to the practical question that must be faced at the present time: when all cannot be saved, who should be chosen to live and who should be allowed to die?

The first criteria that usually are applied are strictly medical ones. Given the physical and psychological condition of the patient, will dialysis confer significant benefit on him? If dialysis will not be useful on medical grounds, then of course it is quite reasonable to withhold it.

But one must be careful here. It is difficult for a layman to judge, but it sometimes appears that the medical criteria are not always strictly medical. It is possible for them to hide judgments about social worth. One has to wonder, for instance, whether the automatic exclusion of a man because of "uncooperativeness" may implicitly be a judgment about his social worth. If it is, then this judgment should be

CASE NINE

made expressly, and doctors are not the only ones qualified to make it.

In the beginning, when dialysis was in its infancy, the medical criteria were aimed at selecting good research subjects. Now they are generally expanded to include anyone who will be an acceptable patient. In fact some doctors today claim that they can dialyse anybody. In any event, with the broadening of the strictly medical criteria there are more medically acceptable patients than can be accommodated on the machines. The result is that in an estimated forty-two dialysis centers in our country patients are selected for treatment on the basis of their social utility. Usually a lay committee is set up to make this evaluation and selection anonomously.

Selection on the criterion of social worth or utility is not without precedent. In 1943 there was a shortage of penicillin among the United States Armed Forces in North Africa. It was needed to treat the victims of venereal disease and the victims of battle wounds. The decision of the Theatre Medical Commander was to give the penicillin to those wounded in brothels rather than to those wounded in battle. The reason justifying this decision was that those

Distributing Sparse Medical Resources

wounded in brothels could be more quickly restored to fighting capacity. Ability to make war was the most urgent need and best served the common good.

Triage in disaster medicine follows the same principle. Those most in need of help are quietly set aside, and attention is given first to those who can quickly be restored to functioning, since everyone's efforts are needed in the common purpose of survival.

In these cases the necessary goals are easily focused, and social worth and usefulness can be realistically measured. But life is rarely like that. In our pluralistic society we do not have one or several focused goals or a clear consensus on what sort of life or person is worth more to society than another.

In investigating what actually happens when committees select patients for medical treatment on the basis of social worth, David Sanders and Jesse Dukeminier, Jr., found "a disturbing picture of the bourgeoisie sparing the bourgeoisie," and remarked that "the Pacific Northwest is no place for a Henry David Thoreau with bad kidneys." One wonders how much chance an artist or composer would have before most committees compared

CASE NINE

with a mother of five children. As one man remarked, "A candidate who plans to come before this committee would seem well-advised to father a great many children, then to throw away all his money."

The point I am trying to make is that when a society's goals are not simple and focused, attempts to choose who should live and who should not on the criterion of social worth or usefulness will seldom be successful, especially since cultural values are not the same as genuine social values and the nearly total estimate of the value of a man's life which has to be made will necessarily be filtered through the biases of those enlisted to make the choice.

Another option, which is in use in many dialysis centers, is random selection, either by lot or more usually on a first-come first-served basis. There is legal precedent for random selection of those to be saved when all cannot be saved. It is the rule in United States maritime law. In the *United States v. Holmes* it was ruled that in the desperate situation of an overloaded lifeboat the decision on who should be saved and who abandoned must be made by lot. It was argued that a lottery is the only way

Distributing Sparse Medical Resources

which avoids arbitrariness and shows respect for equal rights to life.

My first reaction to the plan of selecting patients for dialysis by lot was that it was a cop out, an abdication of the human responsibility to make a hard rational decision. At worst, I thought, it was a superstitious pretense of leaving the decision in the hands of God; at best, it was decision by refusal to decide at a time when the best possible human decision is called for. If either of these is the mentality behind random selection, then of course it is unconsionable. But that does not have to be the mentality. There is, I think, a deeper and wiser principle here.

Random selection of those to be saved when all cannot be saved cuts to the heart of the issue. It says that a human person is of transcendental value, that the value of a human life transcends one's usefulness or social worth. On this deeper level all lives should be respected equally, and each one given an equal chance. Random selection by lot or on a first-come first-served basis is the only fair and equitable way.

Therefore as a general policy I think that

CASE NINE

strictly medical criteria should be applied first: Is the patient an apt subject for treatment? No judgment should be attempted about his social worth either implicitly in the medical opinion or openly by a lay committee. After some have been screened out on medical grounds, selection should be made randomly, on a first-come first-served basis or by lot.

I do not say that this rule is absolute; few things are. But as a general policy I think it is the most honest and fair. It is founded in the belief that the true value of a man's life cannot be calculated in utilitarian terms, that at its deepest level every human life has a meaning which transcends its usefulness and social worth, and that as a matter of fact even a man's social worth can seldom be rightly measured in a pluralistic society with unfocused values and goals.

Case Ten

Teenage Petting

Titius, a sophomore in high school, during a CCD discussion on premarital sex, asks if the Church still teaches that petting is a sin.

The past teaching of Catholic moralists, supported on several occasions by decrees of the Holy See, was that even incomplete sexual acts by unmarried persons are mortal sins. Technical language put it this way: *nulla parvitas materiae in re venerea*—there is no small matter in sexual sins. This meant that any deliberate thought, word, or deed engaged in for the purpose of sexual arousal no matter how slight was always gravely sinful for an unmarried person. Hence kissing, petting, touching, danc-

CASE TEN

ing, hand-holding, hugging, reading, thinking, or speaking that is done to arouse any venereal pleasure is a serious sin outside of marriage.

It did not mean that all these activities were mortal sins in themselves but only if done for the purpose of sexual stimulation. If they were done for some other legitimate purpose they were permitted on two conditions: a person must not internally consent to the sexual stimulation that occurs and he must have a sufficient reason proportionate to the risk that he might consent to the pleasure aroused.

The common casuistry was governed by the principle of double effect. According to a usual example in the moral theology textbooks, when a seminarian reads a textbook on the morality of sexual acts there are two effects— the knowledge necessary for a priest to hear confessions, which is a good effect, and some sexual stimulation, which is a bad effect. If the seminarian does not consent to the venereal pleasure (and, it goes without saying, does not intend it to begin with) then he has a proportionately serious reason for studying the text.

The same principle was applied to kissing, dancing, touching, and so on: does one have a sufficient reason to permit some involuntary

Teenage Petting

sexual stimulation? If so, his action is lawful; otherwise it is not. And under no circumstances and for no reason may he ever consent to or "take pleasure in" any sexual arousal without being guilty of mortal sin.

The casuistry became quite detailed. Moralists sorted out the various parts of the human body into *partes honestae* (the good parts of the body), *partes minus honestae* (the less good parts of the body) and *partes inhonestae* (the bad parts of the body). The bad parts were the genitalia, and the less good parts included the female breasts, upper arms and thighs, and perhaps a few other areas, depending on the strictness of the author.

One, of course, needed a less serious reason to touch the good parts of the body and a more serious reason to touch the less good or evil parts. Hand-holding could be justified in honest, clean dancing, whereas touching the genitalia could be justified only by serious medical necessity like surgery. In 1929, when one Dutch theologian published a more lenient opinion, his book was ordered withdrawn from circulation. One thing was clear, the Holy See insisted: *nulla parvitas materiae in re venerea.*

It is true, there are areas in which there can

CASE TEN

be no parvity of matter where every violation is grave, for instance where any degree contains a substantial violation, as in perjury, blasphemy, or hatred of God, or where the matter is indivisible, as in homicide or adultery. And there are other areas where some violations of the law are substantive or grave and some violations are trivial or slight; theft, for example, can be a grave or a slight injustice. Traditional Catholic morality argued that sexual pleasure fits into the first category. Incomplete sexual pleasure, it was argued, is of its very nature an organic part of an indivisible whole: any sexual actuation, even the most insignificant and transient, tends of its very nature to the perfect or complete act of orgasm. The moral reasoning therefore was this: the complete sexual act outside marriage is gravely deordinate; but the incomplete act is designed of its very nature to form one organic whole with the complete act; therefore the incomplete act is also gravely deordinate. Hence, *nulla parvitas materiae in re venerea.*

This reasoning of course can be questioned. It has been questioned by some few Catholic moralists in the past and is being questioned by many in the present. Very little has appeared

Teenage Petting

in print so far, but I think it is fair to say that among contemporary moralists there is at least a solid and probable doubt about the validity of the traditional teaching and that a more lenient opinion admitting slightness of matter in sexual sins is solidly probably and can be safely followed in practice.

Pastorally, however, it would be a mistake simply to go to young people with this information, telling them that many modern moralists no longer teach that petting is a mortal sin. I do not mean that the pastor of confessor should hide this information from them out of fear that they will abuse it. Rather I mean that it would be an inadequate way to educate them in this important and delicate matter.

It is not useful merely to substitute contemporary casuistry for traditional casuistry and think that one has educated Christian consciences. It is important to instruct teenagers in the disvalues and problems associated with petting in such a way that they can personally appropriate a full understanding of the human and Christian significance of sexual activity. Out of this understanding they can make important practical decisions about their own sexual and interpersonal behaviour. Specifi-

CASE TEN

cally, two things should be emphasized: (1) limited sex is like limited war: it tends to escalate; and (2) petting frequently is exploitative and depersonalizing and so trivializes and falsifies the true meaning of human sexuality.

First, sexual actuation does tend of its nature to orgasm. It is difficult to sustain the traditional argument that incomplete stimulation is an organic part of an indivisible whole so that there is no slight matter possible here. But it is an obvious biological fact that sex is like Cracker Jack: the more you eat the more you want. Sexual arousal is progressive. Rather than satisfying, incomplete stimulation creates an appetite for more. It is admittedly possible for a couple to stop petting at an incomplete stage. But that is often more of a frustrating than a rewarding experience. And one is kidding himself if one thinks that there is never any danger of "going all the way."

Second, kissing or petting may in some instances represent the relationship that exists between the couple. But in many instances it does not. Rather it is nothing more than the selfish exploitation or reification of another person for the sake of one's own sensual gratification.

Teenage Petting

There is probably no other area in which rationalization and self-deception are more common than here. If kids resist these cautions, the counsellor should not be surprised nor deterred from his insistence on them. Kids are only kids and do not have all the wisdom. They need to learn how good sex is, that it has a deeper meaning than sensual pleasure, and that its abuse trivializes a very important human value. The question that they must learn to ask is not: How far can I go without commiting a mortal sin? The question is: What is appropriate behavior for me? What behavior truly represents my relationship and commitment? It will take some ruthless honesty for them to answer it properly.

Case Eleven

Clerical Obligations: Celibacy and the Breviary

Titius is a seminarian in second-year theology. He will be ordained a deacon next year and is apprehensive about the two obligations he will have to assume with the diaconate—perpetual celibacy and the daily recitation of the Roman Breviary. At the present time he believes that at least for him celibacy is possible and will be extremely useful for an effective ministry. But he is conscious that many of the men in the classes ahead of him believed the same thing but later changed their minds and got married. Personally he wants to make a sincere,

CASE ELEVEN

permanent commitment at ordination, but he is not sure in this swiftly changing world how he will feel about celibacy five or ten years from now.

Also, Titius has tried saying the breviary and has found it a useless form of prayer for him. He already dreads the burden of its daily recitation under force of Church law. He knows that many priests do not say the breviary any more but feels that it would be hypocritical for him to overtly assume the obligation at ordination without any real intention of fulfilling it.

1. *Celibacy.* The present policy of the Catholic Church, both in the East and in the West, is never to allow priests to marry and continue to exercise their priesthood. And it is the policy in the West, at least in normal circumstances, not to ordain married men to the priesthood. This policy reflects a long and ancient tradition, and it is most unlikely that the Church will substantively modify it in the forseeable future.

There is no necessary connection between celibacy and priesthood. There is no evangelical precept or intrinsic reason compelling the

Clerical Obligations: Celibacy and the Breviary

Church to maintain this policy forever. Celibacy and priesthood are two different things, and it is possible for a man to have a vocation to one and not the other.

Nonetheless, the Church has linked the two by canon law. And it is important to understand that although the connection between celibacy and priesthood is not necessary, neither is it purely juridical. That is to say, the connection is not simply a legal one, as if the law requiring celibacy for priests were wholly arbitrary. There is a natural affinity between the two, a certain appropriateness or suitability which does not demand but strongly suggests the present discipline.

This is principally what Pope Paul VI tried to explain in his encyclical letter, *Sacerdotalis Coelibatus*. Briefly, celibacy has a three-fold significance—Christological, ecclesiological, and eschatological—which makes it most appropriate for priestly ministry. By the Christological significance the pope means that since the priests of the New Testament share in the priesthood of Christ, it is fitting that they reflect him in his ministry as closely as possible. This means that the priest ought to imitate him in his celibacy, which indicated his

CASE ELEVEN

single-minded dedication to the loving service of God and all men. The ecclesiological significance of a celibate clergy is the freedom and flexibility to dedicate oneself wholly and exclusively to the service of the Kingdom. And the eschatological significance is the sign of the presence on earth of the final stages of salvation and the stimulus to the pilgrim people to look to what is above and to come.

The Church does grant dispensations from the obligation of celibacy. The commitment that a man makes at ordination is not an absolute one. It cannot be. Only an absolute being can effect something that is absolute. A vow is a promise about the future, but many of the contingencies of the future remain hidden from us. The Church or any human power cannot make a law which binds absolutely in all possible situations. Neither can an individual legislate for himself, as it were, by a vow in any absolute way. He will change in ways that he cannot foresee and so will his circumstances. Sometimes this change will result in a personal situation in which he cannot and should not remain a priest. Even if the Church did not give dispensations there would be situations in which an individual would not only be

Clerical Obligations: Celibacy and the Breviary

permitted but obliged to get married without a dispensation, making use of epikeia. For if there is a conflict between the good and the law, a man is bound always to the good, not to the law.

But to say that the Church can, does, and should give dispensations from celibacy after a man has committed himself to it at ordination and to say that no man can make a truly absolute commitment is not to tell the whole story.

While the Church does grant dispensations after ordination, she requires and expects a total, final, permanent commitment before ordination. Although this commitment cannot be permanent in any absolute sense, it is permanent *humano modo,* in a human sense. To say that there are no absolute commitments among human beings is not to say that there are no commitments. Nor is it to say that none of them is in any way final, permanent, and binding. A promise is a promise and demands fidelity, even though there may be extraordinary circumstances in which its binding force breaks down. It would certainly be dishonest to feign this promise from the beginning and wrong to go back on it when one encounters difficulties. Celibacy is not only a gift; it is also a task and a goal always still to be achieved.

To put this another way, a priest is obliged to celibacy by both a juridical bond and a moral commitment, and these two are not the same thing. The Church can dispense from the juridical bond, but she cannot touch the moral commitment. That is between the individual and God. It is conceivable that a priest might go through all the proper legal channels and forms and be released from his juridical bond and still be guilty before God because of infidelity to his moral commitment. There are certainly good reasons why a priest may not be obliged any longer to his original moral commitment, so much so that he ought to leave the active priesthood and marry. But it would be a sign not of Christian charity but of heterodox doctrine to whitewash all cases automatically as if there is never any sin involved. Slum landlords and the White House staff are not the only sinners in the world. Priests also can sin, and one of the sins they can commit is infidelity to the commitment they made at ordination.

Titius, therefore, should approach ordina-

Clerical Obligations: Celibacy and the Breviary

tion with this mentality: he is going to make nothing less than a permanent commitment but nothing more than a human commitment. It is admittedly possible that one day it will have to be revoked. And it is certain that it is not a decision which is made once and for all at ordination and then forgotten about. It is a decision that will have to be constantly renewed, deepened, and remade as long as he lives.

2.*The Breviary,* After ordination to the diaconate Titius also will be bound by canon 135 to recite the divine office every day. Like other ecclesiastical laws which enjoin a practice, the gravity of this obligation is to be measured according to the principle of substantial observance: single violations of the law are not grave matter but the substantial or general neglect of it is.

The divine office is the official public prayer of the Church. It is essentially a communal prayer, and its present sturcture developed in the monasteris. In the first three centuries only monks were obliged to attend the choir recitation of the breviary. From the third to the eleventh century the diocesan clergy became

CASE ELEVEN

more organized and the practice developed of reciting the office publicly in the parish churches. Local statutes were enacted which obliged the diocesan priests by reason of their benefice to attend the public or communal recitation in their parish churches if they were able. But if not, they were never bound to private recitation.

In the thirteenth century the Decretals of Gratian established a universal obligation for benefice holders to attend the communal celebration of the office in church. St. Thomas Aquinas defended this law arguing that since a priest has a special obligation to pray he is obliged to attend choir recitation in his church.

But many medieval canonists went further. They argued that a secular priest must say the office privately if he is unable to attend the church service. In practice the parish priests began to say the prayers they liked or knew by heart at the approporiate times of the day.

During the fifteenth century the breviary became popular through the missionary efforts of the Franciscan friars. Often the breviary was the only pious or religious book that anyone had. Hence the custom developed of reading it in private. Whether this custom ever became

Clerical Obligations: Celibacy and the Breviary

law by force of custom or *consuetudo* is arguable, since it is not clear that the priests who began reading the office in private intended to assume the practice as a binding obligation. In any event, it is doubtful whether there was any legal obligation for diocesan priests to recite the breviary privately until the promulgation of the *Code of Canon Law* in 1917.

One cannot take seriously the Quietistic objection that prayer cannot be prescribed or made obligatory. This possibility is entirely consonant with our fallen nature. But an objection that must be taken seriously, if only for the reason that one hears it so often, is that the breviary is not a useful form of prayer for a great many diocesan priests. Some have found it more useful now that they can read it in English, but others say that the English translation has only revealed to them that they were not missing anything before. Many liturgical and scripture scholars today would support the judgment that the divine office even in its revised form is not a suitable form of prayer for many modern priests in the active ministry.

It is not an adequate answer to say that as long as one says the words and intends to pray one is performing a human act and that act is an act of prayer, having a value *ex opere operantis Ecclesiae,* which is a value beyond that of personal meaning for oneself. For unless the prayer is personally meaningful, its ritual performance is a useless and frequently destructive influence in one's own spiritual life. It consumes time that could and would be given to more useful prayer and simply makes one resentful toward Church authorities who place this burden on him.

I think it is fair to say that the substantial intent of the legislation on the breviary is regular daily prayer for the parish priest, and I would think that he is already bound to this by divine-natural law independent of any canonical legislation. Therefore in practice I would conclude that some form of regular prayer is obligatory for all priests and that the substantial or habitual neglect of this obligation is grave matter.

If de facto the Roman Breviary is a suitable form of genuine prayer for an individual priest, then he is obliged to it. But if de facto it is not a useful form of prayer for him but is a mere juridical observance, then he is free and in fact bound to assume some other more appropriate form of prayer for himself. In these circum-

Clerical Obligations: Celibacy and the Breviary

stances there is no need for him to seek a dispensation or commutation of the breviary obligation. All he need do is practice the virtue of epikeia.

In their discussions of epikeia many of the early twentieth-century manualists followed the lead of Suarez, who understood epikeia as the benign interpretation of the mind of the legislator who is presumed in a particular case not to wish to urge the observance of his law because of special circumstances. St. Thomas Aquinas, on the other hand, did not regard epikeia merely as a reasonable restrictive interpretation of the law but rather as the moral virtue controlling the correct application of the law against its literal sense. The positive law simply asserts what is normative in general and binds in usual cases. But it does not and cannot articulate the true moral good for every instance and in every stiuation. The virtue of epikeia finds the true moral good in the concrete situation in a way that is opposed to the words of the law.

Epikeia, therefore, is not merely a loophole, a way out of moral duty. Rather it is a Christian virtue, and not to practice it when it obliges is a sinful act. That is why the spirit

CASE ELEVEN

gives life and the letter kills: it is possible to sin by observing the words of positive law. For we are obliged to seek out and practice the true moral good in our existential situations, not simply to observe the letter of positive laws. And when there is a conflict between the good and the law, a Christian is always bound to the good, not to the law.

Case Twelve

Devotional Confession

On Holy Saturday afternoon Bertha, a suburban housewife who is a weekly communicant, goes to confession for the first time in two years. After confessing a few venial sins she tells the priest that she used to go to confession every month but does not see any point to frequent confession any more.

It is no secret that the lines in front of the confessionals are shorter these days and that there is a great deal of uncertainty among many Catholics about the meaning and value of frequent confession of venial sins.

CASE TWELVE

The meaning and special value of devotional confession is clear enough in the theological literature. The following summary of contemporary thinking may be of some use to the priest in explaining this matter to the people.

First of all, we must admit that the traditional reasons given in favor of frequent confession—spiritual direction, forgiveness of sins, and increase of grace—are not able to explain its special meaning and value. It is true that spiritual direction, for instance, can be given in the sacramental forum and in fact has an important place there. But it also can be given outside and independent of sacramental confession and often with better effect. Therefore spiritual direction cannot be alledged as the proper function and special value of devotional confession.

Neither is forgiveness of sins an adequate explanation of the special meaning of frequent devotional confession. Imperfect contrition is required as a necessary disposition for sacramental forgiveness of venial sins. But imperfect contrition is sufficient for the forgiveness of venial sins even outside of the sacrament. Therefore it seems that our venial sins are already forgiven in every case before we receive sacramental pardon. One can hardly be motiva-

Devotional Confession

ted to receive an optional sacrament by an effect which is already had without it. What is more, according to the Council of Trent, the Eucharist brings pardon of our "daily sins." And since the Eucharist is a sacrament of the living and Penance a sacrament of the dead, it seems that it is the Eucharist which is directly aimed at overcoming those sins which retard rather than kill the supernatural life of grace.

Neither is an increase of grace a good explanation of the proper identity and special effect of devotional confession of venial sins. For an increase of grace is an effect which is common to all the sacraments and one that can be had extrasacramentally.

The special meaning and value of devotional confession is that it brings not merely pardon of sins but sacramental pardon. Over and beyond the mere forgiveness of sin sacramental forgiveness adds three things. One is a clear and dramatic manifestation of the gratuity of God's forgiveness. A man who in the privacy of his room examines his conscience and is sorry for his venial sins is forgiven by God. But the reception of sacramental absolution in a confession of devotion visibly demonstrates the important truth about all forgiveness—that it is not the work of the good repentant sinner but

CASE TWELVE

of the free God of grace, who brings about in the repentant sinner even his own acts of repentance.

Another thing that the sacrament adds is a visible manifestation that the grace of forgiveness, like all grace, is a free, unique, historical break-in of God. Forgiveness is not given to man by a transcendent, always merciful God according to some general univocal law. It is the free action of God showing mercy to whom he will show mercy, incalculable, unpredictable, unique, and historical. This truth is visibly accentuated in the sacramental event.

Finally, sacramental confession also signifies and effects not only pardon by God but pardon by the Church. Since even venial sin is an offense against the Church, devotional confession has a special meaning in that it is a visible sign of a man's reconciliation and deepening communion with the visible Body of Christ.

These three things identify the specific value and meaning of frequent confession of venial sins. But exactly how frequent devotional confession should be cannot be decided in a univocal or mathematical way. In each case the judgment will have to be made by an individual according to his own devotional needs.

Case Thirteen

Price Control and Demand Control

Titius, a junior executive at General Motors, works in the comptroller's office. Recently he has become disillusioned about the company's pricing policy. He has discovered that its policy is in principle noncompetitive. Although there is no open collusion with the three other giants in the industry, there is a tacit agreement throughout the industry to charge a common price. Although controlling prices by tacit covenant is not clearly in violation of antitrust laws, Titius feels that it is certainly unethical. One evening the local parish priest stops over for a drink and in the course of the conversation Titius explains the problem

CASE THIRTEEN

to him and questions what he learned in the seminary about a just or fair price.

The conventional wisdom assumes that the fair price is determined in the marketplace by the law of supply and demand. In a free-enterprise system all goods and services are auctioned off, as it were, to the highest bidders. Thus, the market price—which is the fair or just price—is set by an invisible hand.

That was the view and the language of Adam Smith. Free competition is essential for the process to work. The only danger, therefore, is a monopoly or a collusion of competitors to fix prices above the fair price that the free market would have determined. Prices established above this by monopolies or monopolistic practices are unfair or unjust. They are exploitative of the consumers because they are not set by an invisible hand but by human manipulation inspired by greed. Such is the conventional wisdom which has formed the basis for our current antitrust legislation and our textbook moral theology.

In modern industry the broad, open, competitive market still exists in some places. Take for instance the garment industry. Although

Price Control and Demand Control

there is already an unmistakable movement toward a takeover by large manufacturers, small business still dominates the industry. It is a big market—over $16 million in 1970—but it is dominated by small businesses—about 21,000 establishments. Most of these are single-shop operations employing about fifty to a hundred people. It is also a highly competitive business. Almost 20 percent close down or move out of New York City each year. And because so little capital is required to begin a business—enough to buy a few sewing machines and hire a handful of women—a comparable number of new businesses are always being started.

Because his industry is so highly competitive the garment maker operates in a market where the prices adjust quickly, easily, and impersonally to supply and demand. There are so many manufacturers, each producing so small a part of the total supply, that no one can either raise or lower the market price and still remain in business. If a manufacturer asked more than the market price, he would find no takers and his business would go to his competitors. And if he lowered the price, he would not increase his volume of sales because he is already pro-

CASE THIRTEEN

ducing up to capacity and can sell all that he can produce at the market price. To take less than the market price would simply lower his profits, put him out of business, and leave the market price unaffected. Therefore in a "price-taker's market" such as this, to ask the moral question, "What is a fair or a just price?" is to ask a meaningless question. There is and can be only one price, and that is set by an invisible hand.

But that is not the whole story or even the principal story about modern industry. Small business is not dead. But big business is bigger than is commonly appreciated. Of more than $1.3 trillion in business sales during 1970, the top twenty-five corporations accounted for 14 percent, the top hundred for 23 percent, and the top five hundred for 36 percent. General Motors is not merely the world's largest automobile company. It is five of the world's largest automobile companies. In 1970 its sales totaled more than the gross national product of all but the seventeen largest industrial nations in the world. It is no surprise therefore that there is no great number of competitors anxious to enter the field. No one would be foolish enough to try. The great industrialist

Price Control and Demand Control

Henry J. Kaiser tried it after World War II. Not only did he fail, but two established competitors, Hudson and Studebaker, were also forced to leave the field. The result is that presently the domestic automobile market is shared by only four companies and dominated by three.

The point is that this is not atypical in our modern economic society. What is becoming atypical is the garment industry, and even here the very recent trend has been toward centralization. In 1971 in some sectors of the industry the fifty largest firms accounted for one-fifth to four-fifths of all sales.

The growing phenomenon in modern industry is domination of a market by a handful of firms. Presently four firms dominate the markets for primary aluminum, copper, rubber, cigarettes, soap and detergents, whiskey, heavy electrical gear, structural steel, cans, computers, aircraft engines, sugar, biscuits, pig iron, iron, tinplate, trucks, and a host of other items. Such is our modern industrial system. It is what modern economic theory calls oligopoly. This is not monopoly, which is wholly uncompetitive. But neither is it a free, broad, and open market where prices are set by an invisible hand.

CASE THIRTEEN

The fact is that in an oligopoly competition is the last thing that affects price. The difference between a monopoly and an oligopoly is that in an oligopoly there is competition. But there is no competition in price-making. No matter how intense the competition, there are some things that men do not do if at all avoidable. In ancient warfare cities were destroyed and populations slaughtered. Almost any form of barbarism was tolerated. But everyone knew not to poison wells! All may be fair in love and war, except what would spell final disaster for everyone involved.

The one thing that big business cannot withstand is a price war. If one firm in an oligopoly has enough resources to outlast his competitors in a price war and so could destroy his competition, he would still stand to lose because the government breaks up monopolies, and so the victorious firm also would be destroyed. But even more importantly, big business is so big that to operate efficiently it needs a great amount of time and capital. This means that big business requires industrial planning, and industrial planning requires that prices be predictable and under control.

Big business has much to gain, but it has

Price Control and Demand Control

much more to protect. In order to protect its enormous investment it has a top priority, the mitigation or elimination of every risk. Popular myth has it that all business is risky, but that is not true of the large modern corporation. Big business has been highly successful in eliminating uncertainty and risk. "Little ventured, little lost," has become sound corporate policy. This is not an indictment of big business. For just as a high level of production is necessary for economic security, a high level of economic security is necessary for maximum production and profit. Big business can be run efficiently to the extent that all risks are minimized and the future is predictable. Big business can be run efficiently only if industrial planning is possible, and industrial planning is possible only if prices are under control.

In spite of the widespread myth that is given credence in our political rhetoric and antitrust legislation, prices in the modern oligopoly are effectively and systematically managed. The management of prices is not achieved by monopoly or by overt collusion. Rather it is achieved by tacit covenant. For example, one of the four firms sharing a particular market, say, United States Steel, will calculate the price

CASE THIRTEEN

most beneficial to all in the industry. It will then announce the price increase, but only because its management is fairly certain that the other three firms will follow suit. Everyone, including the government, knows what is going on, but there is no attempt to invoke anti-trust legislation.

John Kenneth Galbraith analyzes the matter in *The New Industrial State:* "The mature corporation has taken control of the market . . . to serve not the goal of monopoly but the goals of its planning. And the planning itself is inherent in the industrial system. It follows that the antitrust laws, in seeking to preserve the market, are an anachronism in the larger world of industrial planning. Reform of the antitrust laws must wait, however, until the action is illuminated by this far larger fact. The process by which it will come, it may be mentioned in passing, will follow a fairly predictable course. Devotees of the market and friends of the antitrust laws are not lacking in intellectual commitment and even passion. They will respond to suggestions that these laws are largely unrelated to the modern scene with vigor and, on occasion, with indignation. They will note that such questions have been

Price Control and Demand Control

raised before, sometimes by those with a frivolous view of the problem, sometimes by those with a special reason for wishing exemption from the laws. These men, on the whole, will dominate the argument. But circumstance will be on the other side. And that, as always, will prove a decisive handicap. After much discussion, the laws will one day be accommodated formally to the reality. In the meantime the convention by which they exist but are not enforced is by no means intolerable."

In some rare cases collusion is necessary to control prices. And since the management of prices is so crucial to big business, it is not surprising that collusion is attempted if necessary. In the early 1960s executive officers of General Electric, Westinghouse, Allis-Chalmers, and Ingersol-Rand, all manufacturers of electrical equipment, were prosecuted for conspiracy to fix prices of certain heavy electrical equipment. The price-fixing was for transformers and switch-gear which are built to specification and sold, in part, by sealed bids. There was no common price for these items, and price competition presented a serious danger to the industry. The motivation for the collusion to fix prices was not simply a desire to increase

CASE THIRTEEN

profits. Rather, it was that the normal opportunity for tacit regulation of prices was missing. The difference was that here collusion was necessary whereas usually it is not. And that is how they ran afoul of the antiturst laws, even though everybody knew that the prices of electrical motors, washing machines, refrigerators, and other household appliances were also fixed, not by overt collusion, but by an industry-wide schedule which all companies followed as a matter of course.

Those who are aware of this fact in our modern industrial society often conclude that big business manages prices for its own avaricious gain, that it uses its power over market prices to charge more than it could obtain in a truly free, open, and competitive market. And so it exploits the public by using its monopolistic or, more precisely, its oligopolistic power to charge an unfair or unjust price.

Many economists today claim that this conclusion is false. For, they argue, the price that will in fact produce the greatest profit for the corporation is no different in a market dominated by a few concerns from that in a market shared by thousands of firms. In both instances the price that will yield the greatest profit is identical: it is the price that will produce the

Price Control and Demand Control

greatest volume of sales at the lowest unit cost.

It is this price that the marketing department of any big corporation seeks to find. It tries to calculate as exactly as it can what volume at what price will make the greatest profit. The higher price does not always bring the greater profit; it may reduce sales and lower profit. A fully competetive market is known as "a price-taker's market," and an oligopolistic market is known as "a price-searcher's market." The best price, the one that will actually produce the greatest profit, is the same in each. Therefore the price-searcher's market searches in its own interest for the price that would prevail in a fully competitive market. The calculations will be inexact but can be reasonably close, and it is in the selfish interest of big business to get as close as it possibly can. For to the extent that it misses, it loses profits.

What this means is that even in an oligopoly the ethical question—What is a fair or just price?—is an irrelevant and useless question. There is only one price that anyone wants, and it is the very price that in a fully competitive market would have been set by an invisible hand.

Other economists dispute this analysis. They

CASE THIRTEEN

argue that in a fully competitive industry new competitors continue to enter the field and so keep profits down to the "fair rate of return" needed to keep the industry going. But this is not so in an oligopolistic industry. Here it sometimes pays management to restrict its buying or selling, because in this way it can lower the price at which it buys or raise the price at which it sells. Hence the oligopolistic industry does not always produce the ideal volume from the point of view of society's wants.

The fault of monopolies or oligopolies therefore is one of omission. The oligopoly does good but does not do enough of it. To increase its profit an industry sometimes restricts production, even though it could make a satisfactory profit, one which would keep it in business, by expanding production. The result is that big business makes more money than it needs for an acceptable profit. The consumers pay more for the product than they would have to, and some consumers do not buy the product at all, using their money for some other purpose.

I cannot tell for certain which economic analysis is true. But even if the second one is

Price Control and Demand Control

correct, the ethical judgment cannot be too severe. In an affluent society almost all consumer goods can be described as luxuries, not necessities of life. I would resist a moral conclusion that every manufacturer has a strict moral or social duty to satisfy everyone's preferences for goods as long as it can do so without losing money.

Besides, I do suspect that the first analysis is the correct one. It is more in accord with modern economic theory about the nature and goals of the mature corporation. The mature corporation is primarily interested in growth and expansion, and it subordinates all else to this goal. Its concern, therefore, is not to get the highest rate of return on its investment in the short run. Its concern is to make quantitatively the greatest profit possible. This means that the mature corporation aims at setting a price which is described in the technical language of economics as genuine and correct. A price is genuine when it clears the market, and a price is correct when it equals the marginal cost. This happens to be the price which automatically and mechanically would be found in a fully competitive market.

One may be tempted to conclude from all

CASE THIRTEEN

this that in the matter of price-making in our modern industrial society there is no useful moral question to be raised. What is a fair or just price? is not a meaningful question. Whether prices are set impersonally in an open and competitive market like the garment industry or humanly controlled and managed in an oligopoly, there is only one price that everyone wants because it is in the best interests of all concerned. There is no "fair" or "just" price. There is only a price that is genuine and correct.

Now, I believe that this analyis is right. If the proper conclusion from it were that no meaningful moral question can be raised, that would be useful enough to know. But it would be a mistake to conclude that this analysis eliminates the moral question. Rather, I believe, it locates the moral question more exactly.

The moral problem arises, it seems to me, not in price control but in demand control. Industry cannot manage prices without also managing demand, and it is here that some ethical problems arise.

John Galbraith has described this other side of the coin: "Control of prices is for a pur-

Price Control and Demand Control

pose—for the security of the technostructure and to allow it to plan. But price control does little to advance these goals unless there is also control over the amounts that are bought or sold at these prices. Security, growth and effective planning would be jeopardized by erratic or unpredictable price behavior. But these would equally be frustrated by a decision by the public not to buy at the controlled prices. ... So intimately intertwined with the need to control prices is the need to control what is sold at those prices. The control or management of demand is, in fact, a vast ... industry in itself. It embraces a huge network of communications, a great array of merchandising and selling organizations, nearly the entire advertising industry ... and other related services and much more. In everyday parlance this great machine ... [is] said to be engaged in selling goods. In less ambiguous language it means that it is engaged in the management of those who buy."

This is especially true in our affluent society where most of our needs are not elementary physical ones like food, shelter, warmth, and so on. Most of our needs are psychological in origin and so are easily created or manipulated.

CASE THIRTEEN

Hence it is that so much advertising appeals to our need, not for the product, but for personal achievement, social acceptability, equality with our neighbors, sexual fulfillment, personal beauty or an orderly peristalsis according to some standard established not by nature but by a priori canons.

The principal effect of the tens of billions of dollars spent on advertising is not to gain for one competitor more of the market than for another. The competitive effect is minor. Competing ads for Ford or Chevrolet, Winstons or Kents, Alka-Selzer or Bromo-Selzer, cancel each other out. One company does not win nor does it want to win. Each company's advertisements serve to insure it its share of the market. But the major effect of all the advertisement is to maintain the market itself in which all can share. The major effect is crucial for the entire industry: it must convince people of their need to spend a certain portion of their income on automobiles, cigarettes, or antacids.

There is a lot of frivolous literature today which mocks or condemns the whole advertising enterprise. But because one is annoyed at commercials for Dristan or Charmin is no reason to unfairly indict a whole industry. It is

Price Control and Demand Control

a simple fact that the advertising industry is necessary for our economic society to survive. Without advertising, the industrial machine would break down and our economy would come apart with a general decline in employment and our standard of living. Therefore, unless one opts for the destruction of our modern industrial society, he must acknowledge the moral right, in fact the duty, of the technostructure not only to produce a supply of goods and control their prices but also to control and manage a massive demand for them.

But one does not have to admit its right to do this in any way it pleases. A number of issues could be raised here, but I will only raise the one I think is most critical.

Modern business does not always discover needs and then produce the goods or services to satisfy them. More often it creates in people new needs or wants by means of advertising, and these needs are not always what will be of genuine benefit to the people. For instance, a great deal of money has been spent to make human beings afraid of smelling like human beings. And so they are now being sold chemicals to reduce their human smell. Of course

CASE THIRTEEN

once people do not want to smell like people it is quite legitimate to manufacture and sell them chemicals which will cure them of that smell. To cure men and women from smelling like men and women serves a human want, makes them happier, and so is a service to them. But the creation of the need was a disservice. After people have spent their money in satisfying their new need they are no better off than they were before that need was created. Creating useless needs and wants in order to make a profit in satisfying them seems clearly a social disservice and scarcely morally justified. A fortiori this is true if the need created is not only useless but harmful like a craving for cigarettes.

A deeper issue along the same lines but one very difficult to get at in any useful or practical way is the problem of creating in people new needs of wants even when they can be defended as in some way beneficial. One has to wonder if the industrial revolution was such a boon to mankind as is commonly believed. I do not mean to endorse some simplistic back-to-nature theory. But greater concern for the trap we have fallen into might help to extricate us from it, or at least help to keep us from

Price Control and Demand Control

getting in deeper. Left to its own natural momentum the industrial complex keeps creating new needs or wants in people so as to expand and expand production. Sometimes one feels that we are like the squirrel running up the spinning wheel and turning it with the same movements. Much of our industrial society is going fast but going nowhere. What we need is greater concern for a more human hierarchy of values than is provided by the natural inertial movement of a technostructure which of itself has no other value or goal than its own growth and expansion.

FURTHER READING

CASE 1. VASECTOMY AND ARTIFICIAL INSEMINATION

Dedek, John F. "Remaking Man," *Human Life*. New York: Sheed and Ward, 1972 (pp. 98-109).

Fried, John J. *Vasectomy*. New York: Saturday Review Press, 1972.

Häring, Bernard. *Medical Ethics*. Notre Dame: Fides, 1973 (pp. 90-94).

Van Allen, Roger. "Artificial Insemination (AIH): a Contemporary Re-analysis," *Homiletic and Pastoral Review* 70 (1970), 363-372.

CASE 2. INVALID MARRIAGES IN THE INTERNAL FORUM

Bassett, William W. (ed.). *The Bond of Mar-*

riage. Notre Dame: University of Notre Dame Press, 1968.

Dedek, John F. "Divorce and Remarriage," *Contemporary Sexual Morality.* New York: Sheed and Ward, 1971 (pp. 139-161).

Kelleher, Stephen J. *Divorce and Remarriage for Catholics.* New York: Doubleday, 1973.

"The Problem of Second Marriages: An Interim Pastoral Statement by the Study Committee Commissioned by the Board of Directors of the Catholic Theological Society of America." *CTSA Proceedings* 27 (1972), 234-240.

Wren, Laurence G. (ed.). *Divorce and Remarriage in the Catholic Church.* New York: Newman, 1973.

CASE 3. BAPTIZING CHILDREN OF LAX CATHOLICS

Daniélou, Jean S.J. "The Church of the Poor," *Chicago Studies* 4 (1965) 137-146.

Rahner, Karl, S.J. "The Present Situation of Christians," *The Christian Commitment.* New York: Sheed and Ward, 1963 (pp. 3-37).

CASE 4. ASSISTING AT ABORTIONS

Ad hoc Committee on Pro Life Activities, National Conference of Catholic Bishops, "Pas-

Further Reading

toral Guidelines for the Catholic Hospital and Catholic Health Care Personnel," Washington, D.C.: United States Catholic Conference, 1973.

Dedek, John F. *Human Life.* New York: Sheed and Ward, 1972 (pp. 5-90).

CASE 5. HOMOSEXUALITY

Curran, Charles E. "Dialogue with the Homophile Movement," *Catholic Moral Theology in Dialogue.* Notre Dame: Fides, 1972 (pp. 184-219).

McNeil, John J., S.J. "The Christian Male Homosexual," *Homiletic and Pastoral Review.* 70 (1970), 667-677; 747-758; 828-836.

Weltge, Ralph W. (ed.). *The Same Sex.* Philidelphia: Pilgrim Press, 1969.

CASE 6. SUNDAY MASS

O'Callaghan, John, S.J. "Christian Conscience and Laws of the Church," *Chicago Studies* 11 (1972), 59-72.

CASE 7. CHEATING THE INTERNAL REVENUE SERVICE

Galbraith, John Kenneth. *The New Industrial State.* New York: The New American Library, 1967.

FURTHER READING

Lerner, Abba P. *Everybody's Business.* New York: Harper and Row, 1961.

Nikolaieff, George A. (ed.). *Taxation and the Economy.* New York: Wilson, 1968.

CASE 8. PASSIVE EUTHANASIA

Dedek, John F. "Euthanasia," *Human Life.* New York: Sheed and Ward, 1972 (pp. 119-142).

Kelly, Gerald, S.J. "Preserving Life," *Medico-Moral Problems.* St. Louis: The Catholic Hospital Association of the United States and Canada, 1958 (pp. 128-141).

Ramsey, Paul. "On (Only) Caring for the Dying," *The Patient as Person.* New Haven: Yale University Press, 1970 (pp. 113-164).

CASE 9. DISTRIBUTING SPARSE MEDICAL RESOURCES

Ramsey, Paul. "Choosing How to Choose," *The Patient as Person.* New Haven: Yale University Press, 1970 (pp. 239-276).

Sanders, David and Dukeminier, Jr. "Medical Advance and Legal Lag: Hemodialysis and Kidney Transplantation," *U.C.L.A. Law Review* 15 (1968), 364.

Further Reading

CASE 10. TEENAGE PETTING

Bertocci, Peter A. *Sex, Love and the Person.* New York: Sheed and Ward, 1967.

Curran, Charles E. "Sexuality and Sin: A Current Appraisal," *Contemporary Problems in Moral Theology.* Notre Dame: Fides, 1970 (pp. 159-188).

Dedek, John F. "Premarital Petting and Coitus," *Contemporary Sexual Morality.* New York: Sheed and Ward, 1971 (pp. 19-43).

O'Neil, Robert and Donovan, Michael. "Premarital Sexuality," *Sexuality and Moral Responsibility.* Washington, D.C.: Corpus, 1968 (pp. 121-144).

CASE 11. CLERICAL OBLIGATIONS: CELIBACY AND THE BREVIARY

Dedek, John F. "Celibacy," *Contemporary Sexual Morality.* New York: Sheed and Ward, 1971 (pp. 66-91).

Paul VI. *Sacerdotalis Coelibatus.* Rome, 1967.

Schillebeeckx, E., O.P. *Celibacy.* New York: Sheed and Ward, 1968.

Semple, Martin. "Renewal and Priestly Prayer," *America,* April 18, 1970, pp. 419-423.

FURTHER READING

CASE 12. DEVOTIONAL CONFESSION

Dedek, John F. "The Theology of Devotional Confession," *CTSA Proceedings* 22 (1967) 215-222.

Rahner, Karl, S.J. "The Meaning of Frequent Confession of Devotion," *Theological Investigations III*. Baltimore: Helicon, 1967 (pp. 177-189).

CASE 13. PRICE CONTROL AND DEMAND CONTROL

Galbraith, John Kenneth. *The New Industrial State*. New York: The New American Library, 1967.

Kraus, Albert L. *The New York Times Guide to Business and Finance*. New York: Harper and Row, 1972.

Lerner, Abba P. *Everybody's Business*. New York: Harper and Row, 1961.